Angels Around You

Jolita Penn McDaniel

WESTBOW
PRESS®
A DIVISION OF THOMAS NELSON
& ZONDERVAN

Scriptures taken from the Holy Bible, New International Version®, NIV®. Copyright © 1973, 1978, 1984, 2011 by Biblica, Inc.™ Used by permission of Zondervan. All rights reserved worldwide. www.zondervan.com The "NIV" and "New International Version" are trademarks registered in the United States Patent and Trademark Office by Biblica, Inc.™

Scripture taken from the New King James Version®. Copyright © 1982 by Thomas Nelson. Used by permission. All rights reserved.

Scripture quotations are taken from the Holy Bible, New Living Translation, copyright ©1996, 2004, 2007, 2013, 2015 by Tyndale House Foundation. Used by permission of Tyndale House Publishers, Inc., Carol Stream, Illinois 60188. All rights reserved.

Scriptures taken from the American King James Version of the Holy Bible.

Scriptures taken from the King James Bible.

Scripture quotations are from the ESV® Bible (The Holy Bible, English Standard Version®), copyright © 2001 by Crossway, a publishing ministry of Good News Publishers. Used by permission. All rights reserved.

Scripture and/or notes quoted by permission. Quotations designated (NET©) are from the NET Bible® copyright ©1996-2016 by Biblical Studies Press, L.L.C. All rights reserved.

This book is a work of non-fiction. Unless otherwise noted, the author and the publisher make no explicit guarantees as to the accuracy of the information contained in this book and in some cases, names of people and places have been altered to protect their privacy.

WestBow Press books may be ordered through booksellers or by contacting:

WestBow Press
A Division of Thomas Nelson & Zondervan
1663 Liberty Drive
Bloomington, IN 47403
www.westbowpress.com
1 (866) 928-1240

Because of the dynamic nature of the Internet, any web addresses or links contained in this book may have changed since publication and may no longer be valid. The views expressed in this work are solely those of the author and do not necessarily reflect the views of the publisher, and the publisher hereby disclaims any responsibility for them.

Any people depicted in stock imagery provided by Thinkstock are models, and such images are being used for illustrative purposes only. Certain stock imagery © Thinkstock.

ISBN: 978-1-9736-1540-8 (sc)
ISBN: 978-1-9736-1541-5 (hc)
ISBN: 978-1-9736-1539-2 (e)

Library of Congress Control Number: 2018900650

Print information available on the last page.

WestBow Press rev. date: 2/26/2018

Contents

To my beloved sister, JoAn. She knows why.

Angels around You

Jesus replied: "Love the Lord your God with all your heart and with all your soul and with all your mind."

—Matthew 22:37 (NIV)

Prelude

Eye has not seen, nor ear heard, Nor have entered into the heart of man, the things which God has prepared for those who love Him.

—*1 Corinthians 2:9 (NKJV)*

Just take a long slow breath in, let it out slowly, close your eyes, and go with me, if you will, on a short journey.

Father God, send Your angels with us on this journey, and open our minds to exactly what You want us to see.

Here we go! We are lifted off this planet, past the moon, past the red planet Mars and the brilliance of Venus. Behind us is the rapidly vanishing Milky Way. Far beyond the speed of light, our beautiful blue Earth is disappearing quickly, and for just a moment before it's gone, it appears as a little blue ping-pong ball hanging in the vast, perfect, blue vault of space. Millions upon millions of stars, beyond my ability to comprehend, blur past us as we climb ever higher and higher to the outer spheres of space, the very edge of God's universe.

Do I hear music? Could that be the morning stars singing?

While the morning stars sang together and all the angels shouted for joy. Job 38:7 (NIV)

What an ethereal, unearthly melody! Are these the gates of heaven ahead—clouds shimmering with crystal colors I've never before seen? Can those be the twelve gates of the New Jerusalem? Am I just imagining twelve gigantic pearls glowing in their opalescence?

There is a vast and shining city in the distance, but can you see above the city? Look! Hovering far up into the atmosphere is even way more than I had so hoped to see—angels in white linen, thousands upon thousands of them. Their caroling is majestic and soul satisfying; they are singing a rich, magnificent praise song. They pause from time to time to raise a harmonic, joyous chanting in perfect rhythm praising our good God. I detect an indescribable fragrance perfuming the air, and I feel an overwhelming presence of peace and love.

I am transfixed, stunned; it's more than my mind can bear. The beauty and the transcendence is too much.

Whooosh! I'm back on earth changed, humbled, on my knees in adoration and thankfulness for the knowledge that my hope of heaven is true! I am enchanted. Did you see what I saw? I caught a glimpse of the lovely celestial home. Did you feel the vibrations from the singing stars and joyous angels? Was your heart as touched as mine was?

Thank You Father, for allowing this imaginative journey to enjoy a small view of the place You are preparing for us. I know it is beyond what we can even hope for.

> *The LORD has established His throne in heaven, and His kingdom rules over all. Praise the LORD, you His angels, you mighty ones who do His bidding, who obey His word. Praise the LORD, all His heavenly hosts, you His servants who do His will. Praise the LORD, all His works. Everywhere in His dominion. Praise the LORD, my soul. (Psalm 103:19–22 NIV)*

I can't wait to see our Lord and Savior! I can't wait to see the angels. As I say that, I know angels have always been around me. Have I seen in person one of God's supernatural beings? Not to my knowledge. I give credit to some earthly angels for being some of the most precious persons God has graciously allowed in my life. But the supernatural angels such as Gabriel, who appeared to Mary, and the warrior archangel Michael, I have never seen. I long for them to appear to bring me a wonderful message, and who knows? I may live to see my prayer granted.

Meanwhile, my belief is confirmed by the many times my family and I have been rescued from incidents that nothing but an unseen angel's help could explain.

Psalm 91:1 (NLT) tells us, "For he will order his angels to protect you wherever you go." We know these supernatural beings exist, and what a comfort it is to know God sends them to keep charge over us. I conducted a small study of angels probably forty years ago; how amazing it was to discover all the material available and what our Bible says about them.

I think you might find the following modern-day story about angels fascinating because I surely did. While they were on a scenic drive one afternoon in the back country of northern California, my daughter and son-in-law were stopped and surrounded by a large herd of goats on a narrow road; they were fascinated by the dozens and dozens of types and colors of the goats. They had a long visit with the goat herder; they shared snacks with him, and they found him to be a very personable, interesting, and educated man. They learned he was a Christian and discovered they had a lot in common. "Don't you get a little nervous way back here by yourself?" they asked him.

He told them that he didn't share his story with everybody but that he felt moved to tell them. He was frightened only once when a large group of motorcyclists came roaring down the back road where he'd been encamped. They dismounted, drunk and surly. They became belligerent and threatening while the goat herder remained calm until they started to crowd him in a combative way. He cried out loudly, "In the name of Jesus, help me, Lord!" First one and then all the riders fell back; they looked frightened. Stumbling over each other, they ran for their bikes, started their engines in a panic, and took off in a cloud of dust.

The curious herder turned and fell to his knees. Surrounding his herd as far as he could see were angels standing shoulder to shoulder;

they were sheltering, strong, and protective. He told my daughter and son-in-law that that was the last time he'd ever been frightened.

After my study many years ago, I felt prompted to say, "Angels around you" as well as "God bless you" when I parted company with my loved ones; that's become my habit. It's a comfort to me to know I've asked Him to supply protection for my beloveds, and I trust His mercy and love in granting my prayer. I know He desires no harm to befall any of us. That's how and why I decided to give my book the title it has.

Angels are truly around you, my reader, as you are reading and as you strive to live in goodness and happiness. May my writings uplift and encourage you and point you ever to our Savior and Lord. I want to give you all a few moments, maybe even a couple of hours, of transcendence from the mundane to the holy—the holiness of God's peace, laughter, and triumph. May God's sacred writings infuse your spirit and enrich your daily walk.

> *Rejoice in the Lord always. I will say it again: Rejoice! Let your gentleness be evident to all. The Lord is near. Do not be anxious about anything, but in every situation, by prayer and petition, with thanksgiving, present your requests to God. And the peace of God, which transcends all understanding, will guard your hearts and your minds in Christ Jesus. (Philippians 4:4–9 NIV)*

Opening Prayer

In the blessed name of Jesus, hear my prayer. Open me just as I've opened this new book on this new day, and please write on my pages Your blessed will and sign Your name. Please help me keep my will in line with Your will and bless every word I write. Father God, every day ahead is unspoiled with no disappointments.

With every step I take, please put Your angels around me that I will stay on Your path. As men and women in this world, You know we encounter twists and turns that we sometimes feel powerless to avoid. I ask You, trusting You, that You will never leave us or lead us into anything but the paths of righteousness. Father, as my words are read, give my readers a time of respite from their troubles no matter how terrible they are. Let my words ring true to only Your way, and for those who need it, let joy and hope and enlightenment fill their spirits to overflowing. Father, let the readers be blessed by every word and be directed right to the light of Your love. Hold their hands and please keep Your angels around every step they take. Your will be done always, amen.

Spring

In the seasons of life, I think of childhood through school age as my spring, adulthood to about forty as my summer, and middle age to maybe seventy as autumn. Now in my eighties, I am in the winter of my days. Much of what I have written is true for any season. However, in this section, I have organized my writings by loosely grouping memories, experiences, and encouragements applicable to young people or to parents and grandparents with young ones. Most of my writing can apply to any time of life, but I rather casually separated them into seasons.

Just as tender buds of spring put forth their new growth tentatively, you can count on the winds of March howling and knocking them back and a few storms hampering spring's progress. Inevitably, we watch the full beauty of new leaves and flowers and babies prevailing and replenishing. Soon, spring in all her glory will burst upon us with her energy, beauty, and fragrance.

I see a parallel to life—youth taking baby steps, falling and stumbling, learning to overcome obstacles, and growing into the productive, joyous persons God intended. I see the godly protection I enjoyed in more situations than I can understand or even remember, and I thank God for sending His angels to my family and me.

I hope you enjoy reading and remembering, and I pray you may glean something uplifting to enrich your day.

An Irish Blessing

Just for my pleasure, I am sharing this Irish blessing, author unknown. It is one of my favorites.

> May the blessing of the rain be on you—the soft sweet rain
> May it fall upon your spirit
> so that all the little flowers may spring up,
> and shed their sweetness on the air.
> May the blessing of the great rains be on you,
> may they beat upon your spirit
> and wash it fair and clean,
> and leave there many a shining pool
> where the blue of heaven shines,
> and sometimes a star.

Spring Thanksgiving

I will give thanks to you, Lord, with all my heart; I will tell of all your wonderful deeds.

—Psalm 9:1 (NIV)

Father God, my merciful Father, today, I am filled with gratitude for it's spring, and this new day is pristine, and I just saw two daffodils lifting their yellow heads through the snow, nodding hello to me. The sky is a pale-blue bowl turned protectively upside down. Earlier, a fat, little, bright bluebird baby sat on the deck rail crying out its loudest cheep until its mama came and poked a wiggly worm down its eager, open beak. When they fluttered off together, swooping down the valley, I knew You'd sent me a gift for the day, one I wouldn't soon forget.

The blue sky, the quiet except for the warbling of a meadowlark, the rich aroma of my morning coffee, touches of green peeking through the patches of snow—I get it, Father. You gave me a little gem of peace before I started my day! Thank You, gracious God. In His name, amen.

God's Flashlight

When Jesus spoke again to the people, he said, "I am the
light of the world. Whoever follows me will never walk in
darkness, but will have the light of life."
—John 8:12 (NIV)

So it's 4:53 a.m. I had to get up as usual, and the moon! Oh, the moon is so much—it's hard to find the words, even for me. It's full, huge, and glowing with its familiar soft shadows etched on the surface and hanging low in the sky. Its pale-yellow light is brilliant, radiant against an empty, early morning sky, the color of a lovely, medium-blue canvas. The rolling hills below are quite clear, and the stars are dim except for a couple low in the sky still steadily shining. The beauty pulls me to it like the tides, and I can barely push myself away from the window.

I think of my son, an electrician, driving several hours alone to visit us one night. My daughter, his sister, called him to see how he was doing. His booming voice said, "Oh, honey, I'm fine. The traffic is light, and God's big ol' flashlight is shining on me and lighting my way home!" Now, when I see a big full moon, I think of my son and his apt description of it: "God's big ol' flashlight."

Thank You, Father, for getting my son home to me safely each time, and thank You for the glory of Your night skies!

Unseen Angels

See, I am sending an angel ahead of you to guard you along
the way and to bring you to the place I have prepared.
—Exodus 23:20 (NIV)

All my life, I've felt the presence of angels, though never to my knowledge have I seen one. Years ago after a heartfelt prayer that God would let me witness an angel, I dreamed a clear and beautiful dream about an angel approaching me. But it frightened me so and I was in such awe that I woke up to my dismay. I was very annoyed at myself, but in the scriptures, I find I am not alone; many to whom angels appeared were just as I was—frightened.

The deeper our understanding of God's Word and His plan is, the more aware of His omnipotence and supernatural protection we are, and that knowledge is cause for reverential knee-shaking. The dichotomy is certainly there—as my best friend in this earthly life, He accepts me warts and all, and we walk hand in hand, but the sacred reverence with which I hold Him and His supernatural world is overwhelmingly precious and awe inspiring. I am not thinking of angels every minute of course, but through the years, I have developed an ongoing conversation with Father God that is reassuring and comforting, and the older I get, the bolder I am about talking about it.

Now, Father God, I praise You that You love me and have a plan for me. Open my eyes so I may absorb that plan. Give me and us the heart and desire to continue to walk step by step with You, and let

us see the intelligence and the beauty of the direction You would have us follow. Place within us a passionate desire for the wisdom of trusting You implicitly, but keep us wonderstruck. Thank You for the angels You send, and please keep them around us. In Jesus's name, amen.

On Laughing

Be glad in the Lord, and rejoice, O righteous, and shout for joy, all you upright in heart!

—*Psalm 32:11 (NIV)*

I laugh at things not everyone finds funny. My precious mother used to say to me, "This is not a laughing matter, Jolita!" But when mirth bubbles up and giggles burst forth and overflow, what's a person to do but laugh? Doubled over, gasping-for-breath, tear-dripping, belly laughing is one of the most satisfying moments of life. I think it should be prescribed regularly for better health. God built us to laugh like that.

Don't bother looking for scriptures about Jesus or God laughing; you won't find them. But I started thinking that Jesus said,

> *Let the little children come to me, and do not hinder them, for the kingdom of heaven belongs to such as these. (Matthew 19:14 NIV)*

I can picture little ones clustering around this good man whose heavenly innocence and love they recognize instantly. Some of them are on His lap, and some have their arms around Him. Though it isn't recorded, you can go to the bank on the fact that He smiled at them; it was noisy with a lot of giggles and laughter.

Think about it: Father God, our Creator, maker of all the magnificence of the universe, thought up the duck-billed platypus!

He didn't have to make it look that way. What about the red-bottomed baboon? Tell me those baboons aren't the funniest, especially when they scamper about high in the branches chattering away, their red bottoms flashing here and there! How about clumsy-looking hippos lumbering their enormous bodies about, and giraffes' long necks reaching for impossibly high leaves to munch on or spreading their long legs wide to hunker down and nuzzle their babies. It's the mind of God, His inventive mind, a mind that wanders meandering highways and byways of a thousand times ten thousand inventive thoughts, who created the breathtaking beauty of a peacock with feathers spread in a fan of splendor. He made funny chipmunks to duck in and out of their hidey-holes and flash about like little jerky animated toys. Yes, I think He laughed when He watched them playing and darting in and out.

Today, I watched two small dark birds silhouetted against the bright sky. They flung themselves one after another to tremendous heights, and after stopping midair and hovering for an impossible few seconds, they swooped down at what looked like a heart-stopping free fall, and the chase was on. A mad flashing of wings flying almost faster than I could follow, chasing and diving each other, and I could swear they were laughing!

Suddenly, they were once again up in that high, joyous flight only to fall in that scary free-fall thing and then take off on the chase once more. I thought that God had made that very thing for them to do for their joy, their unfettered joy.

Many scriptures show that God made and approved laughing and a happy nature in general; I've listed a few below.

> A time to weep, and a time to laugh; a time to mourn, and a time to dance. (Ecclesiastes 3:4 NIV)

> Rejoice in the Lord always and again I say rejoice. (Philippians 4:4 NIV)

> Blessed are you who weep now; for you shall laugh. (Luke 6:21 NIV)

He will yet fill your mouth with laughter, and your lips with shouting. (Job 8:21 NIV)

I tell you that in the same way, there will be more joy in heaven over one sinner who repents than over ninety-nine righteous persons who need no repentance. (Luke 15:7 NIV)

Where were you when all the morning stars sang together And all the sons of God shouted for joy? (Job 38:7 NIV)

So while there isn't a recorded verse that says, "God laughed," it is more than obvious He thought up fun, laughter, and rejoicing. What a world it would be without joy, without the pure delight of a baby's wide-open, drooly, toothless smile, or without that quiet, secret smile your loved one blesses you with from across the room.

I finish with that marvelous scripture that never fails to uplift. As you read it, let it sink into your spirit and smile.

Finally, brethren, whatsoever things are true, whatsoever things are honest, whatsoever things are just, whatsoever things are pure, whatsoever things are lovely, whatsoever things are of good report; if there be any virtue, and if there be any praise, think on these things. (Philippians 4:8 NIV)

Straight from the Heart

For where your treasure is, there your heart will be also.
—Matthew 6:21 (NIV)

On Valentine's Day, how I loved the two cards I learned to expect each year from my husband—one a very silly or funny card with his wild exclamation marks all over it, and the other a lovely, sentimental card frankly declaring that I was his forevermore. I knew those cards came from his kind, thoughtful heart.

When they were little, my children lovingly fashioned clumsy and endearing valentines that were keepers, and as they grew older, they brought gifts, flowers, and candy. Friends and family remembered me thoughtfully with gifts straight from their hearts. As a young woman, I began a heart collection because I loved the shape of hearts and the unwritten message they brought me.

And now as I write, I'm thinking of those hearts—on cards, chocolate hearts, candy hearts with sayings on them, shaky hearts drawn with a red crayon, heart-shaped cakes, hand-painted porcelain heart boxes, crystal hearts, gold hearts, and diamond hearts. How very much they meant to me when I received them over the years, but now, the memories they evoke are even sweeter.

But of all the hearts I've collected, the big heart of my prince, the caring hearts of my children, the faithful hearts of my family and friends, and the gentle heart of my Savior are the most precious and beloved.

I got a medical report a few years ago that told me my heart was enlarged. Upon hearing that, one of my nephews Facebooked me this message: "Of course it's enlarged, Auntie Jo, for it's full of the love you've stored up for all of us all these years!" *Purrrrrr.*

The crux of this whole heart thing is love. Christ's life was a daily sacrifice of love even to the end, and love is what keeps this old girl going.

> *If I speak in the tongues of men or of angels, but do not have love, I am only a resounding gong or a clanging cymbal. If I have the gift of prophecy and can fathom all mysteries and all knowledge, and if I have a faith that can move mountains, but do not have love, I am nothing. If I give all I possess to the poor and give over my body to hardship that I may boast, but do not have love, I gain nothing. (1 Corinthians 13:1–3 NIV)*

Thank You, Father God, for Your myriad of blessings, the outward tokens of affection, and the loving hearts of my beloveds so unselfishly given. In His name, amen.

The Blessing of Children

He called a little child to him, and placed the child among them. And he said: "Truly I tell you, unless you change and become like little children, you will never enter the kingdom of heaven. Therefore, whoever takes the lowly position of this child is the greatest in the kingdom of heaven. And whoever welcomes one such child in my name welcomes me. "If anyone causes one of these little ones—those who believe in me—to stumble, it would be better for them to have a large millstone hung around their neck and to be drowned in the depths of the sea."

—Matthew 18:2–6 (NIV)

Speaking of angels, when I was thirteen, my sister gave birth to my beloved niece, my parents' first grandchild. Oh my! The first time I saw her swaddled snugly in her pink-satin bassinette, I was done. As I memorized every curve of that pink, round face, I realized that I was the closest to heaven I'd ever been; my active imagination told me I could feel angels still hovering and watching over her. God allowed them to bring us our very own cherub.

When I was four, my little sister was born; that was the first time I remember my heart swelling to nearly bursting with love. A time came when I was all alone in the room with her. I stood up on the chair and gazed at her as she slept. Adoration was not too strong a word for what I was feeling. I inhaled the sweet baby powder smell, and my yearning to hold her was overpowering. I bent to pick her up; I was frightened to death I might drop her. Even as I leaned over, I remember being aware it might not have been a good idea, but I had waited *soooo* long and had deeply desired too long to hold my baby sister.

I had her sweet, warm heaviness in my arms. I was on my knees on the chair, and I longed to sit down and hold her quietly, but I didn't know how to manage turning around. So still on my knees, I carefully rocked back and forth and put my cheek next to her exquisitely soft, tender cheek, smelled the fragrance of her milky breath, and started humming the Brahms's lullaby Mama always sang to her.

> Lullaby and good night
> With roses bedight
> With lilies o'er spread
> Is baby's wee bed
>
> Lullaby and good night
> Thy mother's delight
> Bright angels beside
> My darling abide
>
> Lay thee down now and rest
> May thy slumber be blessed
> Lay thee down now and rest
> May thy slumber be blessed

Scripture after scripture are about children and the blessing God gives us when He sends them to us. All that is good and compassionate in us wells up in overflowing springs even in the middle of poopy diapers and crying babies who are suffering earaches at 3:00 a.m. All that parenthood asks seems to just come naturally to many—maybe most.

But for some, fatigue, pain of healing from childbirth, lack of sleep, and twenty-four-hour-a-day confinement alone with an infant take their toll. Babies need and demand minute-by-minute escalating into hour-after-hour of hands-on care. It is imperative for new parents to get help even if they find their new roles to be fairly easy. Mothers battling depression especially should seek help immediately—spiritually as well as medically. If ever there was a time when others will understand and be willing to pitch in to help, it is then. New mothers, you have my permission to take care of yourselves. You'll be doing your precious babies a big favor when you stop to put your feet up and drink a soothing cup of tea.

Every day if you can, have a trusted someone (husband, friend, neighbor) watch your baby and take a full hour for a long shower or soothing bath. Lotion and perfume yourself, don fresh, comfortable clothes, and do your hair and makeup. Drink a healthy smoothie that is refreshing and thirst-quenching or a bowl of good soup. Save your own neck!

When my first two children napped, I thought that was the time to catch up on housework, or start dinner, or tackle chores. Wrong! Every time my third child napped, I did too if my other two were safe. That was one of the most important things I did as a mother of three. I left folding diapers (no disposable diapers then) for later, and we ate many quick-to-prepare meals. But we were all happier for it.

Enlist grandparents and even great-grandparents if they're able, for no one loves those little ones more than they do but you and God.

How brief our babies' infancies and complete dependence on us is. Even in one short year, many learn to walk, start talking, and assert independence. Keep in mind that this too shall pass and very quickly. I love this scripture.

> *Like arrows in the hand of a warrior, So are the children of one's youth. How blessed is the man whose quiver is full of them. (Psalm 127:4–5 NIV)*

Father God, bless You for inventing babies and for their infancy and childhood that is uniquely precious. Thank You for their brief time of babyhood so their parents can survive it! Bless the mother reading this that she may find the way to rest and renewal to keep up her strength and remember how much she loves her husband.

Bless the father who might read this and help him in his important role of hands-on helping his wife and being a "benevolent dictator." Please endow both parents richly with Your heavenly wisdom. In Jesus's name, amen.

Summertime in My Childhood

Train up a child in the way he should go, And when he is old he will not depart from it.

—Proverbs 22:6 (NKJV)

Imagine summer, early 1940s, Fullerton, California, school vacation, and in the middle of Southern California's long, hot, lazy days. Mama, Daddy, and my older sister are all at work, and my younger sister and I, just little girls, are at home holding down the fort as Daddy would say. We lived on the 1100 block of East Wilshire, the last block before farming country and miles and miles of orange groves. There were only five small houses on that block and a beautiful persimmon grove across the street whose breathtakingly colorful autumn leaves made up a lot for their worthless, sour fruit.

Those were the years of World War II, and you'd think a second-, third-, or fourth-grade girl wouldn't be worried about war. You'd be wrong in my case. Mama always decreed that I was to watch over my little sister and not to let anything happen to her. Every night after dinner, my father and mother listened to the radio news, and it wasn't pretty. As young as I was, I had absorbed enough that I started fearing we'd be bombed. As carefree as my world was on the one hand, there was that constant threat on the other. When an airplane flew over, I was nearly panicky looking for where I could shelter us; that was a shadow over me that never left for four years. Then there was the day I literally heard the bells ringing out freedom, and an airplane flew over with the enormous welcome letters in the sky proclaiming "Peace."

I was just a slip of a thing then, skin and bones, my daddy said; my blond hair cut in a Dutch bob, shorts and shirt well worn and smudged, fingernails bitten to the nub, bare feet dirty and with nearly always a stubbed toe, calloused soles against the hot cement and asphalt—I was in my element. Our family's definition for *tomboy* was Jolita. While Mama and Daddy were exacting about the behavior they expected of us (and man, we were true believers in their omnipotence), the freedom with which they trusted us on those hot, slow days was marvelous.

We reveled in making our own breakfasts and lunches—exactly what we wanted; maybe pancakes dripping with butter and maple syrup, maybe scrambled eggs, maybe cinnamon toast and homemade hot chocolate. Chocolate chip cookies were a treat, and we just loved making them, though often the weather was too hot for the oven. We were rather young to be trusted with the stove, but woe be to us if we were not cautious and hurt ourselves! Years later, I didn't give my own kids that much freedom.

Lunch was tuna salad sandwiches or PBJs, our made-up recipe of canned chili, tamales, and creamed corn that we still make and love today, and lots of lemonade and Kool-Aid—my favorite was lime. I snitched envelopes of it from the cupboard; we licked our fingers, dipped them in the dry Kool-Aid, and licked them again—yum! Such a treat for a nine-year-old and her five-year-old sister. Telltale red or green always tinted our mouths and fingers for a day after.

We loved the paper dolls Mama bought us and the fanciful wardrobe that grew and grew as I drew the dresses and Jan cut them out and colored them. I think of sitting cross-legged on the warm cement in the shade playing jacks for a solid hour at least. In the worst of the heat, we played Old Maid in the shade, and if we were lucky enough for the ice cream truck to come by, and if we could find a nickel, we'd share a Popsicle. When our neighbor friend Nancy came over and I was free to be by myself for a short time, I would get my latest Nancy Drew book, and avid reader that I was, would read in total bliss all the while keeping an ear cocked for my little sister and her best friend. And of course remaining ever vigilant for enemy aircraft.

When days grew hotter, we'd turn on the sprinkler in the front yard. Half the yard was shaded by the huge tree on the curb, the tree where Daddy had put up the biggest, best swing in our world. When we tired of running through the water, my little sister would lie down on the hot cement and let the sprinkler cool her as it oscillated. I, who always burned, lay on the grass in the shade and relished that cool shower. We would finally get cool enough; the afternoon's heat became more bearable. Sometimes, we'd swing back and forth in that marvelous swing, and we'd squirt each other with the hose; drought was not an issue in those days.

There were five boys on the block who were our ages. Until Nancy and her family moved in and Verlene and her family moved in down the block, it was just us girls and the five hoodlums as Daddy called them. I loved kneeling in the dirt playing marbles with those guys and running races, trying my best to win. I especially loved emulating them running up the old, leaning tree a couple of houses down. It was at an angle so that if you got a good start and were strong and nimble, you could run right up the length of it and be in the canopy in no time. So of course, that's just what we did and spent happy hours surveying our block from the vantage point of that high, green, leafy bower.

Hide-and-seek at twilight was delicious; you could really hide. Neighbors would hear our high-pitched, childish voices yelling, "Olly olly oxen, free, free, free!" or "Red Rover, Red Rover, let (whoever) come over!" That was usually a daily ritual with the hoodlums— wonderful fun. Hopscotch was for cooler hours; we quietly played on the cement driveway as we sat on the grass.

There was a barranca, a flood-control channel, at the end of our short block; it seemed gigantic and other worldly to us, maybe a good twelve or fifteen feet deep. It had been constructed after the 1938 flood in Orange County. It ran under what looked to me to be a huge bridge. (But when my husband and I visited there in the late sixties, I realized that little bridge was so narrow that two cars couldn't pass at the same time.) The barranca, however, was so deep that it was unwise to jump into it, but there were occasions … And what adventure a hike down that channel brought us. Who knew there was hobo village just a mile down in the jungle at the end of the channel? How scary! How thrilling!

A memorable day came; we heard pitiful meowing that led to the rescue of an abandoned tuxedo cat tossed into that deep, dry channel—a tiny, wobbly kitten we named Janjolou—Jan after my sister, Jo after me, and Lou after the little girl I was babysitting at our house at the time. The world of kitties was enchanting for us but the bane of our mother's existence. Fleas, eye infections, and when she grew up, two litters of kittens—a thrill for us but a constant pain for Mama, who absolutely refused to allow Janjolou in the house. But what happy hours we spent with that precious cat and her kittens in the garage and yard.

However, time would always catch up with us; it would be four o'clock before we knew it, and our assigned chores loomed huge in the little time we had left. Besides hand washing and drying dishes, we were to wipe off the stove and slick up the counter tops, sweep the kitchen, take out the trash, make our beds, pick up every bit of anything on the floor and put it away, dust and polish the living room and dining room furniture, and occasionally run the vacuum.

Mama wanted dinner started before she got home, so that meant scrubbing the potatoes and putting them in the oven at 4:30 and cutting up a salad. We always managed to do it, but my word, you should have seen us scramble for our lives when we realized it was four and our parents were due home in an hour.

My children told me that they did the same thing when they were little and I was on the way home. Those daily responsibilities held us in good stead all our lives; we developed a work ethic that never let us down.

I think of today's children and all their accouterments—dozens of electronic things, play dates, and organized activities. I wonder if they're not missing the freedom that in those far-away, long-ago days let us just be kids who came up with our own fun, imaginative games. The busyness and organized activities of today's children make me long for country living, home schooling, and a simplified life. I'm all for piano lessons, exercise classes, and play dates, and I for one adored my elementary years in public school, but I yearn for today's children to have long hours to themselves to choose and maybe explore the garage and pull out old boxes to build a castle.

Okay, back from the 1940s to 2017. What a long, rich life God gave me, and now, much of my life these days is enjoying day after day of peace that brings back lots of memories. I hope today's reading brought back lovely childhood memories of your own and helped you connect even more with your grandchildren and great-grandchildren. We can tell them stories about the olden days, and they can show us how to run our computers!

Father, thank You for those long-ago days of peace and happiness and for my protected childhood. Thank You for Your angels who saved me from many mishaps. Now, Father, please be with those whose childhood memories are maybe not as good as mine, maybe even nightmares, and please deal with them that they may be comforted and gain peace of mind in You. Help us who have grandchildren to create loving, happy memories for them. In Your blessed name, Your will always be done, amen.

Colors in My Life

In my vision I saw what appeared to be a throne of blue lapis lazuli above the crystal surface over the heads of the cherubim.

—Ezekiel 10: (NLT)

My favorite color is blue—all blues. From the day I discovered turquoise in my new box of crayons, blue has always been it for me. That ocean aquamarine—a clean, fresh blue with its tint of green—enchants me. The blue of all my children's eyes proclaims "beloved." Robin's egg blue always takes me back to Mama's shining, warm, and welcoming kitchen. The sky blue I get lost in, in the backgrounds of a myriad of cloud shapes, is pure and pristine—a beautiful spring canopy over my head.

Tiffany blue speaks of elegance and anticipation. Soft, pure, baby-powdery blue makes me melt. Royal blue brings back the time of a luxurious, blue-velvet sheath dress with bright-blue satin trim I wore as a young woman, and, yes, I truly felt royal in it. Navy—I love its subtle, dark strength that subdues and quiets without swallowing the light, and its promise that the light is near.

As a painter, I appreciate all the colors God made for us to enjoy, but somehow, blue is my foundation. Cool and calm and tranquil. Imagine my delight when I came across the scripture describing the lapis lazuli throne of heaven—sapphire blue in some translations. It thrills me to think of colors unknown that God has waiting; there's no telling what He has in store for us.

In painting, you often use a no-color color that's hard to describe because it's so nondescript. But I soon learned how important that no-color was since it was the foil that made other colors sing. Sort of like the dark that makes the bright next to it even brighter. As you learn to see the depth and layers of God's color creation, you might be surprised that you can eventually pick out maybe ten or more colors (often blues) in the leaves of a tree that you may have once described as green.

Thank You, my Father, for creating the unique beauty of blue and of a technicolor world and bringing life out of what might have been only black and white. Help us see all You have for us to see and to always seek and find the beauty. Thank You, our most gracious Creator. In His name, amen.

I Call Him God

But if from there you seek the Lord you will find him if you seek him with all your heart and with all your soul.

—Jeremiah 29:13 (NIV)

For God so loved the world that he gave his one and only Son, that whoever believes in him shall not perish but have eternal life.

—John 3:16 (NIV)

Years ago, someone told me that he didn't believe in God. He was someone I cared about though our friendship was new. It hurt me that he was depriving himself of the most important area in life to develop and nourish himself and his family in loving, healthy, and supernaturally elevating ways. He had no hope of heaven because he claimed to not believe in it.

My response was, "Father God allows your free choice in believing in Him or not. That's up to you. It's just so hard for me to understand that as intelligent as you are, you don't believe in Him." He said he wondered that as intelligent as I was why I could believe in Him. It turned out that the age-old questions of death and injury, bad things happening to good people, his personal tragedies, and a professor in one of his first college classes who threw the Bible across the room without immediate consequences from God had conspired to dislodge his earlier shaky faith.

I'm no Bible scholar. I don't pretend to know all the answers, nor do I intend to compete. I am still learning. My belief is based on early teaching and then growing in personal experiences, simple study, and commonsense questions. Believe me, I have asked Him many questions myself in our ongoing conversations. However, the faith born in me those many years ago has remained unshakable and has grown even in the face of unspeakable tragedies. I have been in the storm; I have been close enough to the gates of hell that I heard Lucifer laughing, but God was right there with me. He never left me alone. When fear threatened, He pulled me out of it, and I lived to smile again.

Here are some of the few questions I asked myself all those years ago, the answers to which helped solidify my belief.

- Where did all nature come from?
- How were the seasons so perfectly timed as to be self-regulating and self-renewing millennium after millennium?
- Why does the ocean come so far and know to retreat just so far?
- The planets move within their orbits timed to the second with incredible precision—who ordered that?
- The conception, gestation, and birth of human beings are miraculous in themselves; who designed our amazing bodies and their ability to self-heal?
- Where did we get our souls, our spirits, and our inborn need to worship?
- How? Who? Why?

I heard a preacher say that creation could not have been an accidental coming together because how could perfection happen spontaneously? How many times would you have to throw the inner workings of a watch up in the air before they came together and landed all working in perfect harmony? There has to be a universal Creator, an omnipotent intelligence. There is. I call Him God.

The Bible teaches that nature itself worships its Creator.

Blessed is the king who comes in the name of the Lord! Peace in heaven and glory in the highest! Some of the Pharisees in the crowd said to Jesus, "Teacher, rebuke your disciples!" "I tell you," he replied, "if they keep quiet, the stones will cry out." (Luke 19:38–40 NIV)

But ask the animals, and they will teach you, or the birds in the sky, and they will tell you; or speak to the earth, and it will teach you, or let the fish in the sea inform you. Which of all these does not know that the hand of the LORD has done this? In his hand is the life of every creature and the breath of all mankind. (Job 12:7–10 NIV)

I include here the entire Job 38 (NIV) because God Himself was speaking about creation and questioning Job after he got whiny with Him. I'm also including it because it sends chills up my spine and I love reading it again and again. Read it now and you'll want to read it again.

Then the Lord spoke to Job out of the storm. He said: "Who is this that obscures my plans with words without knowledge? Brace yourself like a man; I will question you, and you shall answer me.

"Where were you when I laid the earth's foundation? Tell me, if you understand. Who marked off its dimensions? Surely you know! Who stretched a measuring line across it? On what were its footings set, or who laid its cornerstone— while the morning stars sang together and all the angels shouted for joy?

"Who shut up the sea behind doors when it burst forth from the womb, when I made the clouds its garment and wrapped it in thick darkness, when I fixed limits for it and set its doors and bars in place, when I said, 'This far you may come and no farther; here is where your proud waves halt'?

"Have you ever given orders to the morning, or shown the dawn its place, that it might take the earth by the edges and shake the wicked out of it? The earth takes shape like clay under a seal; its features stand out like those of a garment. The wicked are denied their light, and their upraised arm is broken.

"Have you journeyed to the springs of the sea or walked in the recesses of the deep? Have the gates of death been shown to you? Have you seen the gates of the deepest darkness? Have you comprehended the vast expanses of the earth? Tell me, if you know all this.

"What is the way to the abode of light? And where does darkness reside? Can you take them to their places? Do you know the paths to their dwellings? Surely you know, for you were already born! You have lived so many years!

"Have you entered the storehouses of the snow or seen the storehouses of the hail, which I reserve for times of trouble, for days of war and battle? What is the way to the place where the lightning is dispersed, or the place where the east winds are scattered over the earth? Who cuts a channel for the torrents of rain, and a path for the thunderstorm, to water a land where no one lives, an uninhabited desert, to satisfy a desolate wasteland and make it sprout with grass? Does the rain have a father? Who fathers the drops of dew? From whose womb comes the ice? Who gives birth to the frost from the heavens when the waters become hard as stone, when the surface of the deep is frozen?

"Can you bind the chains of the Pleiades? Can you loosen Orion's belt? Can you bring forth the constellations in their seasons or lead out the Bear with its cubs? Do you know the *laws of the heavens? Can you set up God's dominion over the earth?*

"Can you raise your voice to the clouds and cover yourself with a flood of water? Do you send the lightning bolts on their way? Do they report to you, 'Here we are'? Who gives the ibis wisdom or gives the rooster understanding? Who has the wisdom to count the clouds? Who can tip over the water jars of the heavens when the dust becomes hard and the clods of earth stick together?

"Do you hunt the prey for the lioness and satisfy the hunger of the lions when they crouch in their dens or lie in wait in a thicket? Who provides food for the raven when its young cry out to God and wander about for lack of food?"

An incredible read.

As I taught my children, so what if there wasn't a God and all creation had just happened? But the Bible itself was available for direction. Think about this: the truths, the health advice, the moral living code, the entire setup of civilization is perfectly laid out for us in the scriptures. If we all followed the biblical teachings of the New Testament even without belief in God, would we not all be healthier, happier people? The bonus and the truth is this: God is, was, and always will be. Even more, He is our personal God, our Father, and He loves and cares for each one of us.

The Lord is not slow in keeping his promise, as some understand slowness. Instead he is patient with you, not wanting anyone to perish, but everyone to come to repentance. (2 Peter 3:9 NIV)

"For I know the plans I have for you," declares the LORD, "plans to prosper you and not to harm you, plans to give you hope and a future." (Jeremiah 29:11 NIV)

This is the good news the angels proclaimed that night those many eons ago.

> *Just then, an angel of the Lord stood before them, and the glory of the Lord shone around them, and they were terrified But the angel said to them, do not be afraid! For behold, I bring you good news of great joy that will be for all the people Today in the City of David a Savior has been born to you. He is Christ the Lord! (Luke 2:9–11 NIV)*

He is here today for us right now, miraculously here with me as I type, and amazingly there with you as you read.

Thank You, Father. Hallelujah!

And how about my friend? All these years later, I still call him friend. In fact, I care more about him now than ever. He still proclaims nonbelief, but through our few conversations, I realize he is more agnostic than atheist. Yes, I still pray for him and his family because they are precious people, God's beloveds. I know God's door is open, and it will still be his choice and strictly between him and God. I know too what the scriptures teach—every believer and unbeliever will bow before Him and confess His name on that last day.

> *Being found in appearance as a man, He humbled Himself by becoming obedient to the point of death, even death on a cross. For this reason also, God highly exalted Him, and bestowed on Him the name which is above every name so that at the name of Jesus every knee will bow, of those who are in heaven and on earth and under the earth, and that every tongue will confess that Jesus Christ is Lord, to the glory of God the Father. (Philippians 2:8–11 NIV; emphasis added)*

Father God, our great Creator and Father of us all, You know

my friend, You know his family, and in Your great power and mercy, again I ask please open the door to give this good man and his loved ones an opportunity to choose You. Father, be with my readers; let Your words be meaningful and enrich their lives, and let them choose You. In Jesus's name, Your will be done, amen.

Pray without Ceasing

Rejoice always, pray without ceasing, give thanks in all circumstances; for this is the will of God in Christ Jesus for you.

—1 Thessalonians 5:17–18 (ESV)

As a little girl newly committed—baptized at age nine—as children do, I took things literally. I was learning to pray by listening and absorbing whatever I could. My examples at church usually were long, formal prayers I mostly didn't understand, and they sometimes came from old men who seemed to me to be fossils themselves praying about unfamiliar things. But Daddy always said grace before meals and simple, heartfelt, humble, short prayers—effective learning examples. My standby as a very little girl was "Now I Lay Me Down to Sleep." Jesus Himself gave us the Lord's Prayer as the example for us to use, and for many years, that was the prayer I prayed—the perfect prayer.

Eventually, I found 1 Thessalonians 5:17–18 that urges us to pray without ceasing and to give thanks in all circumstances. *What's that all about?* I asked myself. Praying without ceasing and giving thanks in all circumstances were enigmas to me. But as I matured, I learned that I was to discipline my mind and stay under God's influence in all circumstances. Eventually, praying became as easy as breathing. Praise Him! That's exactly what happened.

By the time I was a young mother, I realized my walk with God was entrenched for life, and I looked for every chance to impart this same connection to my family. At first, my out-loud prayers felt and sounded awkward to my ears, but soon, my conversations with Him became more relaxed and natural. Because I wanted my children to know Him, it became my habit in the car to pray, "Thank you, Father, for this vehicle, and keep us safe as we travel." That short prayer comforted me and was usually followed by another one while I scrambled around trying to get out of the car fast enough to herd my little scattering tribe—(no seat belts to strap them in then), "Father, in your mercy, keep your angels safely around my little ones, help them to listen, and keep me from yelling in the grocery store!" I began to thank Him continually, often aloud especially in front of my kids. Walking with God took on a new meaning for me; when you talk with Him consistently and make Him your confidant, He will become your best friend, and walking and talking with Him will become natural.

Early in my young womanhood, I read Norman Vincent Peale's *The Power of Positive Thinking*. Those pages sunk into my spirit and took root there many years ago. Positivity and encouragement oozed from its pages. A specific decision from Dr. Peale's own life resonated with me; he wrote that he loved to walk along the street and in his mind, just between God and him "shoot" prayers at passers-by. He started smiling at everyone he walked by and was struck by the number of sad faces he encountered. That's when he started shooting prayers, and he took great delight in throwing out these silent seeds of goodwill; he just trusted God to take care of the planting and growing part. That felt like something I could do, and I immediately and happily put it into practice. I am rarely out and about anymore, but all these years later, when I have the opportunity, I shoot someone with an inner prayer, and that tickles me inordinately!

I found that giving thanks in all things is often difficult. One morning years ago in Santa Barbara, I was looking out of the window of the rehab facility I was in following a stroke. I was praying, and I heard in my mind, *Give thanks in all things*. Oh my! I told God I wasn't thankful for the stroke and asked His forgiveness if I was wrong. But I was so grateful to see the gorgeous, intense colors in a single, large, beautiful bird of paradise blossom right outside my window.

That morning, the orderly asked if I wanted anything special, and because the rough sheets were chafing my skin, I asked him if he could use soft flannel blankets as my sheets, and he did. Oh was I ever thankful. I was also so grateful for the nurses' station being right outside my door so that every time I called them, they popped in very promptly.

I wept with gratitude over my husband and our daughter for three weeks of driving 120 miles round trip every day to spend the day with me to assure I was well looked after. I felt very loved, and it was easy to thank God for these comforts in my very changed and different life. If we look for it, we can always find something to be grateful for in every circumstance.

One of the most satisfying times in my married life was when my husband and I started praying together; it took a few years for that to happen. He didn't commit fully to God until his later years though he was a wonderful man who came regularly with us to worship services and approved of his family serving the Lord. In the last months of his life, his wholehearted, selfless prayers for me and our family were some of the dearest words I've ever heard.

It is a thrill to me that my sons and daughters pray at the drop of a hat and that their simple, heartfelt prayers display their comfortable relationship with their heavenly Father. When one of my daughters lived with me, often first thing in the morning I could hear her throw open her upstairs window and holler, "Good morning, Lord!" That always made me smile. Her desire and ability to pray started when I encouraged my children to talk with their Father at early ages. As a toddler, when she was asking the Lord's blessing on our food, she asked Him to bless her baby brother's "baba" in the crib. So endearing.

Prayer might be new to you or difficult, but it's one of the easiest and quickest forms of worshiping Him you can do. Your prayer is yours, and God made you, your thinking, and your language, so you cannot say anything He doesn't already understand about you. Just talk with Him; tell Him that this morning's sunrise was exquisite! God loves a grateful heart. Ask Him to remove anything that may hinder your prayer by forgiving anything that needs it, even perhaps a forgotten misdeed. By your humbling yourself and just uttering simply, "Help me, Lord," you will enter a holy place, the place where He dwells with only you, and He will sanctify you during your time together.

Since Father God knows us before we even formulate our words to Him, praying is as much for ourselves as it is for Him because it organizes our thoughts and zeros us in on our daily priorities. It reminds us to stay elevated mentally and spiritually, and it keeps our connection with the divine constant.

Keep your prayers in your comfort zone. Father God has made it easy for you. You are not required to learn written prayers, though in the past, I have learned some that were wonderful. The Bible gives us the perfect example in the Lord's Prayer of keeping it simple, and we don't need to preach a sermon.

> And when you pray, do not be like the hypocrites, for they love to pray standing in the synagogues and on the street corners to be seen by others. Truly I tell you, they have received their reward in full. (Matthew 6:5 NIV)

I have a little formula I made up and used before I became comfortable with praying regularly: PRAY is an acronym that works for me, and it might work for you too.

P—Praise and thank Him.
R—Repent.
A—Ask for requests.
Y—Yield your life to Him again and again.

In winding up their prayers, most New Testament Christians follow what Jesus instructed and how He prayed Himself. In John 14:13–14 (NIV), Jesus said, "And I will do whatever you ask in My name, so that the Father may be glorified in the Son. If you ask Me anything in My name, I will do it."

And so before our "amen," we obediently ask, "In the name of

Jesus." Again, "Father God, not my will, but Your will be done" is the example Jesus gave when He prayed in Gethsemane. I almost always include this affirmation to help me to align my will with His.

So if praying is not a familiar and comfortable part of your life, you are losing out on a valuable, powerful asset. Ask that He give you the desire and ability to pray, and voila! He will, and before you even realize how easy it has become, you will be there. Believe me, I know.

Father God, thank You that You have made Yourself instantly available through the means of prayer, and praise You for a thousand blessings You continually shower upon me and mine. Now be with those who may struggle with conversations with You, open that door wide for them, and bless them with the happiness and joy that come from talking with You that You gave me so many years ago. Give me wisdom in my words, Lord, to encourage the desire to pray without ceasing within those who haven't experienced such a blessing. In His name, always Your will be done, amen.

As a Man Thinketh

For as he thinks in his heart, so is he.

—*Proverbs 23:7 (AKJV)*

I think this verse is probably the third most important verse in the Bible, the first and second, of course, being these.

Jesus replied: "Love the Lord your God with all your heart and with all your soul and with all your mind. This is the first and greatest commandment. And the second is like it: Love your neighbor as yourself." (Matthew 22:37–39 NIV)

What motivates me, what upsets me, and what calms me is what I let into my mind and heart. God has intertwined our bodies, minds, and spirits so that just the thought of a baby's smile instantly affects our mood. Remembering a beloved's hug and kiss and loving words is much like stepping onto the beach and breathing in a lungful of negative ions—that recharges my being. On the other hand, the thought of a huge tax bill hanging over my head makes that sense of well-being plummet, and a TV program showing someone dying often brings me right back to the tragic moment my beloved left me, and I am poleaxed.

Father God provided so much variety, so much beauty, such soaring music, a myriad of positive things in this world knowing there were hard days ahead for us. Flowers, wonderful fragrances like bread baking, the breeze in the trees, a river view, the vast ocean panorama, catchy or lyrical music, a loved one's smile or touch, a hearty laugh, a comfy bed, and a child's arms around our necks are a few reminders of His care that helps us balance the tough moments with the tender. Our Bible teaches us to think on lovely things as in Philippians 4:8.

> Finally, brothers and sisters, whatever is true, whatever is noble, whatever is right, whatever is pure, whatever is lovely, whatever is admirable—if anything is excellent or praiseworthy—think about such things.

Satan's plan is always to bring us to the dark side, and he uses tricks of ruining daily living with usually small and large irritating things, one right after another—a car breaking down, a dishwasher overflowing, bad news on the phone. Just as tiny beetles can eat away at a mighty oak and eventually bring it down, all these irritants sometimes wear me to the breaking point. Rather often in the midst of chaos, I would go into my closet and yell at the top of my lungs, "Get away from me, Lucifer! I recognize you, and in Jesus's name, I send you back to the pit! I am a child of God!" I always follow with a quiet prayer: "Now Father, fill me with your peace and strength." That's a simple and quick stress reliever, and it works to this day for me; it's my way of following God's plan for fighting off disaster in my thoughts.

Another practical and simple way of diverting negative thoughts is to immediately say, "Stop!" when a negative thought comes to your mind. Immediately think of a soothing memory or whatever fills you with peace. In my mind, I walk on the beach and see a blue sky and an even bluer ocean. I feel the warmth of the sun, I hear the cry of gulls and their fluttering wings above me, and I smell the briny, wet, glistening seaweed. Finally, I scrunch my toes in the warm sand and conjure up a beautiful, pink, curved conch shell to take home. I have found that to be an effective way of quieting and calming my mind.

I have a friend who told me that she sings a hymn immediately when she faces troubling thoughts, and that works for her. Years ago, another friend told me that when she was in the middle of cooking dinner and her little ones were clamoring for attention, she used to take the top off her bottle of vanilla extract and inhale that familiar and delicious fragrance. For her, it was calming and intoxicating. Who'da thunk?

To arm myself with "the breastplate of righteousness" for the day, I read His Word for a few quiet moments while the day is still untouched and I am fresh from the night's respite. The psalms never fail me, and even a short prayer gives me some *oomph*. I'm an early riser, and watching the glory of the sunrise with my cup of coffee and taking the few moments to read and pray make all the difference. When I don't begin the day that way, later, it's harder to find that type of peaceful moment.

God has given us the greatest gift, the gift of our minds that are like the mind of Christ. We have the ability to discern and understand spiritual things, and if we zero in on Him, that ability grows and develops richly and powerfully: *"Who can know the LORD's thoughts? Who knows enough to teach him? But we understand these things, for we have the mind of Christ"* (1 Corinthians 2:16 NLT).

Father God, again in gratitude, I ask You to help us through rough times and to remind us of Your beautiful mind that is free to enter our minds and fill us with the peace and confidence that You will never leave us. In His name, amen.

Summer

Summer is a bountiful, blooming season of life when the newness of love and careers and responsibilities that never occurred to me before burst into a full-grown garden of overabundance—a profusion of fruit and vegetables and blossoms right in my lap to cherish and nourish. All the promise in those planted seeds of spring sprouted and grew and flourished more than I had ever imagined. *Oh my! I am an adult. All this is my bailiwick now, and how do I do it?*

During day after day of sun and heat and long, warm nights, weeds grow, drought takes over, and the fence falls down, but step by step, faltering at times, my muscles of faith grow strong. I welcome the satisfying sense of accomplishment, but I mightily struggle to the point of tears with some of it. However, with God's strength, mercy, and grace and the angels I trust Him to send, I make it.

The Crucifixion and My Epiphany

When Easter approaches, reminders begin about the sacrifice our Savior made for us and His triumphant Resurrection. It is not about the Easter bunny and new clothes and Easter dinner, although believe me, I love that part of the joyous celebration of spring.

More than the superficial, what I appreciate so much is that for a short time—much like during Christmas—at least some of our world is reminded of Jesus, the Son of our Father God, who left heaven for our sakes. It brings to mind Philippians 1:18 (NIV): *"But what does it matter? The important thing is that in every way, whether from false motives or true, Christ is preached. And because of this, I rejoice. Yes, and I will continue to rejoice."*

When my story took place, it was a chilly spring, and the day was quiet except for the cheeping of baby birds and the breeze occasionally rippling through the wind chimes. I was fifty-eight; I had been raised in a Christian home, baptized at age nine, and was a dedicated follower of Christ—and have remained so to this day. I led a somewhat sheltered early life, and it was easy for me to accept a benevolent Father God, His Son, Jesus, and His Holy Spirit. The Trinity was (and is today) a mystery, but one I fully accepted and in which I still believe.

My Bible knowledge and faith included a deep respect and awe for the Crucifixion. It always centered on my amazement at how Jesus could have been so obedient to leave the paradise of heaven, accept becoming a human being, and actually live the perfect life He did especially since He was supernaturally aware of how His life would end. My human nature still finds it incredible that He did that.

Maybe the familiarity of repetition of reading the account of Christ's last days, all the lessons I sat in on (and that is hard to explain), perhaps made me superficially accepting of the story. I knew His sacrifice to be true, and it made me sorrowful, but even as I shuddered when I pondered it from time to time, somehow, I hadn't taken it deep into my soul and spirit. I did puzzle over how God, His Father, could actually bear to send His Son specifically to be sacrificed. But I accepted it on faith and put my puzzlement on the back burner by thinking, *After all, God is omnipotent and can handle anything, and He knew Jesus would end up being back in heaven.*

However, true my rationale was that it seemed rather shallow of me. That quiet afternoon just before Easter, I was once again flipping back and forth between the four gospels and reading all the events surrounding Jesus's arrest, the mockery of His trial, His sadistic humiliation and torture, and finally His Crucifixion and Resurrection. That cool spring day, I came to the passage in Matthew 26:38–40 (NIV).

> *Then He said to them, "My soul is overwhelmed with sorrow to the point of death. Stay here and keep watch with me." Going a little farther, he fell with his face to the ground and prayed, "My Father, if it is possible, may this cup be taken from me. Yet not as I will, but as you will." Then he returned to his disciples and found them sleeping. "Couldn't you men keep watch with me for one hour?"*

No matter that I had read that many times in my life, it began to hit me more fully than ever the dread He was feeling, and more poignantly significant, why He was called the Man of Sorrows. That day, I read online what I judged to be an excellent article by Donald Macleod entitled, "Why Have You Forsaken Me?" It's a long but important read. I quote sections of it here because they explain so much of my eye-opening then and why it became such an epiphany for me on that long-ago day.

And at three in the afternoon Jesus cried out in a loud voice, "Eloi, Eloi, lema sabachthani?" (which means "My God, my God, why have you forsaken me?").

Up to this point, the narrative of the crucifixion has focused on the physical sufferings of Jesus: the flogging, the crown of thorns, and his immolation on the cross. Six hours have now passed since the nails were driven home. The crowds have jeered, darkness has covered the land, and now, suddenly, after a long silence, comes this anguished cry from the depths of the Savior's soul.

The words are an Aramaic-tinged quotation from Psalm 22, and although Matthew and Mark both offer a translation for the benefit of Gentile readers, they clearly want us to hear the exact words that Jesus spoke. At his lowest ebb, his mind instinctively breathes the Psalter, and from it he borrows the words that express the anguish, not now of his body, but of his soul. He bore in his soul, wrote Calvin, "the terrible torments of a condemned and lost man" Institutes, II:XVI, 10). But dare we, on such hallowed ground, seek more clarity There are certainly some very clear negatives. The forsakenness cannot mean, for example, that the eternal communion between the Father, the Son, and the Holy Spirit was broken. God could not cease to be triune.

Neither could it mean that the Father ceased to love the Son: especially not here, and not now, when the Son was offering the greatest tribute of filial piety that the Father had ever received.

Nor again could it mean that the Holy Spirit had ceased to minister to the Son. He had come down upon him at his baptism not merely for one fleeting moment, but to remain on him (John 1:32), and he would be there to the last as the eternal Spirit through whom the Son offered himself to God (Hebrews 9:14).

And finally, the words are not a cry of despair. Despair would have been sin. Even in the darkness God was, "My God," and though there was no sign of him, and though the pain obscured the promises, somewhere in the depths of his soul there remained the assurance that God was holding him. What was true of Abraham was truer still of Jesus: Against all hope, he in hope believed (Romans 4:18).

Yet, with all these qualifiers, this was a real forsaking. Jesus did not merely feel forsaken. He was forsaken; and not only by his disciples, but by God himself. It was the Father who had delivered him up to Judas, to the Jews, to Pilate, and finally to the cross itself.

And now, when he had cried, God had closed his ears. The crowd had not stopped jeering, the demons had not stopped taunting, the pain had not abated. Instead, every circumstance bespoke the anger of God; and there was no countering voice. This time, no word came from heaven to remind him that he was God's Son, and greatly loved. No dove came down to assure him of the Spirit's presence and ministry. No angel came to strengthen him. No redeemed sinner bowed to thank him.

Who was he? He cries out in Aramaic, but he doesn't use the greatest of all the Aramaic words, Abba. Even in the anguish of Gethsemane, distraught and overborne though he was, he had been able to use it (Mark 14:36). But not here. Like Abraham and Isaac going up to Mount Moriah, he and the Father had gone up to Calvary together. But now Abba is not there. Only El is there: God All-mighty, God All-holy. And *he is before El, not now as his Beloved Son, but as the Sin of the World. That is his identity: the character in which he stands before Absolute Integrity. "Jesus did not merely feel forsaken. He was forsaken; and not only by his disciples, but by God himself."*

It is not that he bears some vague relation to sinners. He is one of them, numbered with transgressors. Indeed, he is all of them. He is sin (2 Corinthians 5:21), condemned to bear its curse; and he has no cover. None can serve as his advocate. Nothing can be offered as his expiation. He must bear all, and El will not, cannot, spare him till the ransom is paid in full. Will that point ever be reached? What if his mission fails? The sufferings of his soul, as the old divines used to say, were the soul of his suffering, and into that soul we can see but dimly. Public though the cry was, it expressed the intensely private anguish of a tension between the sin-bearing Son and his heavenly Father: the whirlwind of sin at its most dreadful, God forsaken by God.

Never before had anything come between him and his Father, but now the sin of the whole world has come between them, and he is caught in this dreadful vortex of the curse. It is not that Abba is not there, but that he is there, as the Judge of all the earth who could condone nothing and could not spare even his own Son (Romans 8:32). Now, Jesus's mind is near the limits of its endurance. We, sitting in the gallery of history, are sure of the outcome. He, suffering in human nature the fury of Hell, is not. He is standing where none has stood before or since, enduring at one tiny point in space and in one tiny moment of time, all that sin deserved: the curse in unmitigated concentration.

He stands where none has stood before or since, enduring at one tiny point in space and time, all that sin deserved.

But then, suddenly, it is over. The sacrifice is complete, the curtain torn, and the way into the Holiest opened once and for all; and now Jesus's joy finds expression in the words of another psalm, Psalm 31:5. In the original, it had not contained the word Abba, but Jesus inserts it: "Father, into your hands I commit my spirit" (Luke 23:46). We have no means of knowing what intervened between the two cries. We know only that the Cup is drained and the curse exhausted, and that the Father now proudly holds out his hands to the spirit of his Beloved Son.

How many sermons had I listened to trying hard not to embarrass myself by weeping in public as Jesus's suffering and death were described, and it still affects me deeply. I remember one moving sermon by a beloved minister, now in heaven, who so vividly described the Crucifixion that not a sound could be heard from the audience except for a few smothered sobs. I immediately left after the service that day; I was unable to greet even one person.

Back to the day I was rereading the last days of Christ—it suddenly struck me that my son Mitchell was thirty-three that year—the same age Jesus was when He died. My Mitch, in the prime of life, healthy, strong, happy, laughing, and always busy, was my beloved, vibrant son. I let my mind wander; I thought about how Jesus must have been at that age—how strong and developed His body was as a carpenter using his muscles in that demanding occupation. How undoubtedly He was in the prime of His life, and how cherished He was by his mother, Mary, and surely His family and the apostles. How could God be so silent and forsake His only begotten, most beloved Son? As I read on in Matthew 27:50–52 (NIV), the words of old resonated.

From noon until three in the afternoon darkness came over all the land. And Jesus cried out again with a loud voice, and yielded up His spirit. And behold, the veil of the temple was torn in two from top to bottom; and the earth shook and the

rocks were split. The tombs were opened, and many bodies
of the saints who had fallen asleep were raised.

So there it was. There it had been all along in His Word. God's great, loving, aching heart, the wounded heart that planned the salvation of His children, His shattered emotions, and yes, I believe His deep anger toward sin, all reverberated in a mighty display of thundering earthquakes and darkness, shattering rocks, and a torn temple veil. Just imagine the bodies of the saints raised and walking about! Who could not wholeheartedly believe in that moment as recorded in Matthew 27:54 (emphasis mine), "When the centurion and those with him who were guarding Jesus saw the earthquake and all that had happened, they were terrified, and exclaimed, *'Surely He was the Son of God!'*"

I realized then very clearly that no matter what circumstance presented, never could I be as self-sacrificing as God the Father was; He gave not only Himself but also His only, full-of-life, perfect Son. I began to weep; my mother's heart realized for the first time (as much as my human mind could comprehend) how very much our God, my Father, loved me, us, and all the people of this world as broken and stumbling as we were. It hit me how truly shattering it was to God as His heart was broken watching his only Son, Jesus, take on the sins of the world, be separated from Him, and endure until death the agony He suffered.

Think of it—the omnipotence of God's emotion! How much more did He need to do to make us understand what had just happened and His sorrow at His Son's sacrifice? He caused earthquakes to shake our planet, darkness to fall in the middle of the day, rocks to split, the dead to walk again, and the temple veil to split! He did all that so we sinners could be saved. His love for us is almost incomprehensible.

I thought of my son's arms about my neck when he was a toddler and how I thrilled at each little accomplishment, my rejoicing at my adult son's achievements and successes, and how I loved our strong, loving connection. I remembered vividly how much I had hurt as my son endured asthma and pneumonia, surgeries and broken limbs, stitches, and the agonies that life hands out as a matter of course. How many nights of lost sleep, hospital vigils, and hours I spent in deep prayer for him I couldn't count. The love I have for him will never let me give him up to save the world. I would in deep fear and trembling give myself but not my son. But what my son has endured in his life has never in the slightest degree approached the anguish Christ suffered. As a blood sacrifice in His Crucifixion, Jesus took on the sins of the world. I felt the beginnings of an understanding about how extreme God's love for me, a sinner, and for all of us was and how loath He is to surrender even one of His beloved creations.

I cried for a long time that afternoon because I had finally caught a glimpse of God as a parent—the Father of Jesus and my heavenly Father. I began to understand a glimmer of the suffering the Father of the Son, God Himself, had endured at the passion of Christ.

I don't know if my story conveys to you how much I had been affected that day and how it changed my relationship with my awesome God and even with all humanity. It may seem very simple to you; I realize now it's a simple truth, but it wasn't simple to me then. The depth of God's love for us is still a marvelous mystery to me. However, as remote and powerful as His kingship places Him so very high in the heavens, ever since that day, I feel a different, life-changing closeness in our relationship and in my ability to approach Him, visit with Him, and yet still worship Him. It is so much easier.

I am prayerful that my sharing may reveal something more for maybe even one person who reads this. As painful and tragic as the event of the Crucifixion were, it now resounds joyfully in my memory every time I think of His death and the miracle—He is risen! Shalom.

Dear Father, in the blessed name of the sacrificed and living Savior, Jesus, I thank You for that terrible and wonderful way You made for us to live eternally. While His universe-changing death was so horrific, You made a simple and eternal plan for us to live with You eternally, and saying thank You is so inadequate. The only other thing I have to offer You is my life, and I give You that asking Your help in living it the way You have planned for me. In His holy name, Your will always, amen.

Independence Day

Blessed is the nation whose God is the LORD, the people chosen as his inheritance.

—Psalm 33:12 (NIV)

I just love bands, especially marching bands. For years, every July 4th, my prince and I would watch the Boston Philharmonic and the Washington Capitol Fourth with inspiring military bands and orchestras playing patriotic and military songs.

Today, I watched *The Music Man* for the umpteenth time. The thrill is always there as I see those bedraggled kids blaring out their pitiful music but then magically turning into exactly the hope in all their minds—an incredibly sharp, perfectly performing marching band. I love the crimson and gold uniforms, row after row of musicians marching in unison, the gold of the horns glinting in the sun, the twirling skirts and flashing batons of the majorettes, the drum major strutting, but most of all the music—the loud, stirring marches. Meredith Willson's "76 Trombones" makes me sing these two lines every time: "Seventy-six trombones led the big parade, with a hundred and ten cornets close at hand."

I don't know the rest of the lyrics except for bits and pieces, but the melody stays with me. After we saw the movie the first time, I embarrassed my kids when I would spontaneously break into song pushing the grocery cart with kids trailing farther and farther behind me. Poor kids! Now, my wheelchair hampers me a little.

John Phillip Sousa's "Stars and Stripes Forever" affects me the same way. My sister and I played a rousing piano version of it as a duet when we were young and full of it. She was more demure than I was, but wow, could she ever bang out a mean march when we played it. So much fun. Even now, I still have a yen to play the drums, wear a gorgeous uniform, and with adrenaline pumping, march to a rip-roaring tune. Yes, I would if I could!

The closest I ever came to that was carrying the beautiful American flag for the Fullerton Junior College band when I was a high school freshman, all of five four in height and 115 pounds. I was more than excited to be asked; in fact, I was very honored. That is until I actually put on the royal-blue and gold, heavy, all-wool uniform with a snazzy high hat strapped under my chin, thick, black laced-up, wide men's shoes over two pair of heavy men's socks on my triple-A narrow feet (which were never the same for a month after that). I buckled on the thick leather holster across my chest to hold the very tall flagpole, and then I struggled back and forth in the stiff breeze trying my best to steady that lovely, twenty-five-pound, huge silk flag (with the gold American eagle at the top). I marched five miles in hundred-plus heat in the National City parade south of San Diego. (Several members of the band fell out from heat exhaustion that day.)

Around the first mile into the parade, I realized why no junior college student was carrying that flag. I haven't a clue why I wasn't smart enough to collapse, but no, I stubbornly stumbled through the whole five miles, too proud to call out, "Uncle! Uncle! Take me home. I'm just a little, stupid freshman dying here!"

I must admit to moments of pride and satisfaction as we marched and people applauded, stood up, and put their hands over their hearts. Some saluted, especially the old men, who took off their hats too and looked ever so much as if they were weeping.

Will there be angel bands in heaven? I know that just like the hopeful kids in *The Music Man*, by His grace, we will be transformed. There will be multitudes of voices and choirs and harps and trumpets playing songs to Him so incredibly superior to those of any of the greatest composers on earth. I am expecting my spirit to soar so much that I'll kneel in praise and joy. All of us will be united as one with who knows what ethereal orchestra God has planned. Can you imagine the energy of us all together filling eternity? More exciting than any Fourth of July marching band!

As we get caught up in the parades, the picnics, and the showering explosions of fireworks, may we never forget why we celebrate Independence Day and how we came to be so honored and blessed to live here in this hard-won freedom. May we respect the memory of those who lived and fought and died so our cups would run over under the protection of His grace. May God continue to bless our nation and continue allowing us, our children, and our children's children to live in this blessed peace under our beautiful American flag. I love our flag, and I love this country, where God placed me and mine.

Father God, in Your great protection, preserve our free nation and keep us able to worship You just as You would have us. Change, stop, and forgive those who are tearing down what You set our ancestors to establish for us. Let us as a nation remember that You are our God and that You are the reason we enjoy our safety and freedom. In Jesus's holy name, Your will always be done, amen.

Praises for This Day

You will go out in joy and be led forth in peace; and the mountains and the hills before you shall break forth into singing, and all the trees of the field shall clap their hands.
—Isaiah 55:12 (ESV)

This morning, I was reminded of what I heard my Gramma Sullivan say when I was a girl: "God must've woke up smilin' this mornin'!" because it was a soft and breathtakingly beautiful day. It was filled with that special green blooming everywhere that happened only this time of year.

During the night, I had been gifted with the sight of the solstice full moon in all its brilliance, and I sat for some time just mesmerized by its beauty. The *Almanac* told me that it was the first full moon on the summer solstice since 1948, and I had been privileged to witness it!

Later, at 5:45 a.m., the sun was completely up, and the full, pure light of day was beautifully illuminating the green hills and mountains. When I wheeled myself to the back of the house, amazingly, I saw that beautiful full moon still high enough in the sky to be breathtaking. So I got to witness a rather rare solstice event, the sun and moon in the morning sky at the same time, and I marveled again at our Creator and what beauty He had chosen to make for us to enjoy.

Thank You, Father, for the rare and for the ordinary, for ever-increasing loveliness, and for letting me see it day after day! In His name, amen.

My Angel Gramma

Stand up in the presence of the aged, show respect for the elderly and revere your God. I am the LORD.
                                        —*Leviticus 19:32 (NIV)*

Her white curls blew against her soft pink cheeks, and when she looked at me, she crinkled her soft brown eyes in a blink that said, *I love you.* We were eating ripe peaches, leaning over the sink, the juices running down my seventeen-year-old arms. I asked her, "Gramma, how did you do everything you did with all your kids and then losing Grampa? How did you make it?" She stopped to think for a minute while wiping her wet hands on her much-washed, old-fashioned, homemade apron covering her ample abdomen. Ever reticent, her soft reply was, "I jes' keep on keeping on, I guess." This understatement coming from one of the most godly women I have ever known. Gramma was one of my first living, breathing angels I recognized as an angel. Her influence has never left me.

She fried the most delicious savory pork chops and made the silkiest yummy gravy to go with them that I ever ate. After I graduated from high school, Gramma was living in a tiny, one-bedroom house just a couple of blocks from church and from where I worked. Mama was concerned about her living alone, so I gladly moved in with her for about six months until she moved to be with my aunt. She and I walked to church together, and I just walked down the alley to my work.

It was a blessed time that I cannot thank God enough for. I can just see her today in my mind's eye. She has long, white hair, long enough to sit on. She walks into that tiny kitchen fresh from her morning bath, white hair gleaming and wound into a big bun. The little curls around her face are drying into soft "commas." She picks out a long, freshly ironed, homemade apron, carefully slips it over her head, and ties it in the back. She goes to the little back door, opens it, and looks out. Gramma has the softest, most feminine voice, but she is quite reticent and rarely offers her opinion. Nonetheless, I hear her say, "God must've woke up smilin' this mornin' it's so pretty out."

She delivered eight children, successfully raised seven of them, and took in two of her brother's children to boot. She gave birth to all her children at home in her own bed sometimes with the help of one of her best friends, a Cherokee midwife. My grampa died when she was only fifty-five (I was just a little girl of five), so even though most of their children were grown, she had a long row to hoe alone.

I never knew Gramma to just sit quietly in her chair unless she was reading God's Word. She always had piecework for the next quilt she was working on. Her gnarled, knobby, severely arthritic hands would be curled around a tiny silver needle as she carefully sewed pieces together to form a beautiful work of art and a source of warmth.

She made dozens of quilts in her lifetime, working clear up to nine months before her death at age eighty-nine. Her goal was to give all her children and grandchildren quilts, and Mama said she thought she did just that. I was blessed to receive one quilt and four quilt tops. One of her quilts won first place at the California state fair and earned a large photo of her and it in the *Sacramento Bee* that year.

I never heard a word of complaint from her, nor did my family. Gramma's daily prayer was, "Father, hep me to be a blessin' to someone today, and hep me to not hurt anybody." She was always a blessing and never hurt a soul in her life to my knowledge.

Father, thank You for enriching my life with my own angel grandmother and for giving me the chance to know her. Help me to be more like her wonderful example. In His name, amen.

My Résumé

*Likewise, teach the older women to be reverent in the way
they live, not to be slanderers or addicted to much wine, but
to teach what is good. Then they can urge the younger women
to love their husbands and children, to be self-controlled and
pure, to be busy at home, to be kind, and to be subject to their
husbands, so that no one will malign the word of God.*

—Titus 2:3–5 (NIV)

While I treasured raising children, I called it the agony and the ecstasy. We had three children—a perfect kid, a rebel, and a fence-sitter who checked out both sides, curious about everything.

I had the privilege of enjoying every minute of one beautiful child's life, and this beloved child fulfilled our every hope. Indeed, my existence today is comfortable and beautiful because of this child and spouse. They are extraordinary servants of the Lord.

Our rebel was a beauty, too, and a more different, delightful child one could not hope for. My husband and I reveled in that difference— precocious, gorgeous, fun. But Satan had his way, and we lived through agonies that I will not go into but that I can assure you gave us experiences that covered the gamut of everything no one would ever have wanted. We were scarred by those long years of struggle, but now, you could not ask for a person more devoted to the Lord. My love for my treasured child is mighty and great.

Our third child was a gift, born with the longest eyelashes, a delight who grew into a loving, precious person full of practicality and common sense. He is solicitous and caring; he flew twice to Montana to be with me, and he calls me regularly, which blesses my quiet life. Thank God he is a believer as well.

We had the privilege of raising one grandchild half of his life; what a blessing and challenge that was. He is totally different from my children and other grandchildren and a pure joy. He is a gifted violinist and a balm for my spirit. I continue to pray many heartfelt prayers for him.

Several different ones moved in with us for respite periods to regain balance, and we showered them with love and whatever they needed for as long as they needed us. It was our privilege, and I always felt we had been called to serve them.

Thus, I speak with some authority about being a parent. I don't have a PhD in child-rearing, but, as I said of my mother, I graduated from the University of Life, as she did, and there are pearls in my storehouse of wisdom I think are worth sharing. And I do remember being a child, so I can even speak about childhood though admittedly from the days of yesteryear. My early life was blessed and sheltered though I was disciplined. Our family had its share of bumps in the road, and money was scarce for us, but I was only barely aware of our deprivations.

I was wife to a wonderful husband for fifty-four years, and I learned a lot about reciprocity in relationships. In spite of the inevitable hiccups in our marriage, I learned much about mutual, unselfish love and giving all to a beloved, and then I had to learn about giving him up. I managed to survive the amputation of a beloved part of myself.

Much of what I learned about life came during my twenty-three years as a medical assistant. I loved the nursing part, and I took pride in the medical-secretarial aspect. I loved my patients. I was always very gratified by helping frightened, sick people through rough experiences and giving them the kindest, most thoughtful assistance I could to make them as comfortable as possible.

But this sheltered young girl very early in her womanhood observed the best and the worst of humankind. I witnessed heart-melting, altruistic compassion and care, and I saw degradation I never once imagined was possible. I worked with some of the most conscientious, caring doctors, and I worked with a couple I wish I had never met. Though I was an office nurse and secretary, I was the reluctant participant in helping deliver babies three times, though that was thrilling too. Sadly, I held the hand of one of my favorite elderly patients as he died. I remember praying mightily in my mind for me, my patients, and my doctor during iffy, scary moments, and I thank the Lord He stood by me. Those years gave me insight into a world I would otherwise have never known.

Parenting was one of my life's assignments I loved. I know I did it well. Though I know I could have done even better, I can still empathize and share. The proof of the pudding is my wonderful children. Yes, there were illnesses, injuries, surgeries, hair-raising ambulance rides, and worse. I still don't know why my family had to suffer through some of the yucky and dark events, but I do know that the bigger the threat you are to Satan, the more he will try to take you down. My family and I were servants of the Lord; we were trying our best to walk in His way.

Many books have been written about good people suffering bad things, and some rightly explain that God gave us free choice; He did not create robots when He created us. Sadly, I must admit that at times, we did not make the best decisions. But then there were those nights of all of us snuggling in front of the fireplace in our cozy living room and toasting marshmallows. There were days of watching our kids do cartwheels on our neat lawn my husband kept so trim, and we had the satisfaction of watching them climb the huge willow in the backyard to oversee their world from their little tree house their daddy had built for them.

There was a lot of laughing. There was year after year of school projects and wonderful report cards, graduations from high school and college, weddings, and the reward of grandkids and then great-grandkids. Yes, I have garnered quite a bit from adventures in parenting. Did I make mistakes? Yes, I did, but I thank you, Father, that they all survived.

So if you need to share dark stuff full of pain and chaos, I can understand because I've been in that dark night of pain. My capacity for compassion overflows, and I offer a shoulder to lean on and an ear that will listen. I'm limited now in my wheelchair, but as a child of God, I'm not a pushover. I am empowered with the strongest weapon against Satan that you can own—the power of prayer.

One of my challenges was having a stroke. It was right up there with the agony of a sick child or one of your loved ones in trouble. I was in the hospital for a week and in rehab for three weeks. I had excellent care, the devoted care of my husband, our daughter, who came for six weeks from her home, and months of compassionate therapists. One of the most significant things I remember is being told that my life span was about five years beyond the stroke. They obviously hadn't consulted God on that one; it's been almost fifteen years since then.

If you will allow Him, God will walk with you, and though it feels as if it will kill you, it won't. It will leave scars, and you will be permanently changed. My constant was and is through good times and bad putting God first no matter what happened. Live a godly life and teach your children His precepts and promises. Though I stumbled at times for sure in that respect, it was always my goal.

Angela Morgan, who must have been a fabulous woman, was born in the late 1800s. She wrote the following, part of a favorite poem of mine that speaks to me and describes a part of me that has never been squelched, for which I am grateful: "In spite of war, in spite of death, In spite of all man's sufferings, Something within me laughs and sings And I must praise (Him) with all my breath."

And now I am old; I'm learning about this new road I'm on that I've never traveled before. I can commiserate with the foibles and challenges of old age as never before because I am here. I can identify with my caregivers because I had done that for over five years while I was in my sixties. So if I get preachy, it is with the loving hope that I might share something to make life a little easier for you whatever stage of life you're in. While I am restricted in what I can do, I can still pray, and my prayer is this.

Father, our great heavenly Father, let me pattern my life after You and Your Son's example, and please keep Your Holy Spirit indwelling and strengthening me during my struggles. You promised me You had a plan for me, and though You gave me my free choice, please nudge me to keep me on target. In Your great mercy, please help me never to leave that path, and keep Your angels around me to bring me back if I should stray.

These days, I am sharing some of the words of wisdom You have imparted to me. Keep my words only straight, sure, and true, and let them sink into those who need most what I have to say. Father, loving You with all my heart, mind, and soul is a blessing that grows every day. Thank You for being my Father, and bless my dear readers with everything I've prayed for myself. Please give them exactly what they need individually. In Jesus's name, amen.

A Mommy Moment

Follow God's example, therefore, as dearly loved children
and walk in the way of love, just as Christ loved us and gave
himself up for us as a fragrant offering and sacrifice to God.
—Ephesians 5:1–2 (NIV)

It is her birthday, and I'm back there once again in that faded yesteryear doing one of my favorite things in the world: I tie a big, soft, white satin bow in her golden blond hair that cascades down her back in soft, wavy curls. The little-girl perfume of fresh shampoo, bath soap, and the warmth of her pink, glowing skin surrounds her like an aura.

Her dress reminds me of an old-fashioned girl's for it flows to her ankles. She refuses to wear her shoes, and she can't stand still even for a moment. Her little feet dance back and forth while I patiently juggle her bow. She suddenly throws her little arms around me, arms that are strong and brown from hours of playing in the sun, and says, "I love you, Mommy!" And those soft, poochy lips smooch my cheek with a big, loud smack! I'm a puddle. I'm done. I'm more gratified for this moment in time, this gift, more than any diamonds or gold.

Oh Father, thank You for this moment. Thank You for the warm, little-girl fragrance of her hair and her strong, brown arms. Help me store this preciousness up against the day I become less than her favorite. Open my eyes to all these fleeting loving moments, and keep them imprinted in my storehouse

of treasures to help me remember through the desert days of petulance and short tempers. Please, Father, keep her safe always. Thanks isn't enough, but thanks again, Father. In the name of Jesus, amen.

I am so thankful for the memory. It warms me again and again!

A Special Day

And over all these virtues put on love, which binds them all together in perfect unity.

—Colossians 3:14 (NIV)

We'd been married just a few years, and romance was still bright in my heart. He didn't bring me flowers. It was our day, but he hadn't remembered. I wanted him to remember. He was up and off to work as always, blowing me a kiss as he hurried out.

He came home right on time; the kids ran to greet him and climbed all over him. He said, "Hi, honey," and twinkled his eyes at me. He took out the trash, swept the front porch, and set the sprinkler. "Dinner smells good!" Big smile. He came in with his tools and fixed the catawampus cupboard door that had come off its hinges.

Suddenly, he turned and swooped me up in his arms and asked, "How was your day, sweetheart?" In that moment, I realized that, flowers or not, it just didn't matter. He was the special one, and this was our day. I told him that I had baked him a cake, and he said, "You remembered!" Pulling a slightly crumpled card from his pocket, he presented it to me with a slight bow, and said, "I wondered if you'd remember." Both of us had remembered!

As years went by, we reminded each other in our increasingly busy lives before our special days; that was much more practical in our growing, mutual love for each other than to wait and wonder if one or the other would remember. Our celebrations were low-key, but we always marked them and blessed the day we had met. Sometimes, we had tuna sandwiches that we ate while we read our cards and toasted each other with hot chocolate and a kiss.

But as the money eased up, there were red roses and lovely gifts. Often, we ate at a beautiful restaurant, and he began buying me diamond hearts! But that crumpled-up card from his pocket meant just as much as the diamond hearts he gave me later. They were all from his big, generous, loving heart!

Father, my gracious God, thank You for the day You gave us each other. Thank You that through Your grace, we overcame petty differences and huge slams to our lives. Thank You that through it all, come what may, You gave us what it took to stand shoulder to shoulder to live our lives together.

Thank You for the precious, loving times, for our romance, and for our friendship. Thank You for preserving our marriage for fifty-four years, for sending me the love of my life, and for allowing us to complete our vows of commitment. Thank You especially for granting me peace that he is with You, resting after giving his all for You, for me, and for us. I pray for my readers that their lives may be blessed with at least the same happiness and contentment You gave my prince and me. In Jesus's blessed name, Your will always, amen.

Praises for His Bounty

Let them give thanks to the Lord for his unfailing love and his wonderful deeds for mankind, for he satisfies the thirsty and fills the hungry with good things.

—Psalm 107:8–9 (NIV)

Grocery shopping was always an unwelcome chore; how often I dreaded it. **Thank You, Holy Spirit, for the awakening to see my grocery store in a whole new light.** There before me was not only food for my body but a visual feast as well. The produce department with its deep leafy greens, bright reds, sunny yellows, and the care that the clerk has taken to artistically arrange this lovely produce was obvious. I was suddenly very mindful of this blessing that is too often taken for granted—an overflowing plethora of goodness all mine for the selecting. I was so blessed by the yummy choices and the money I needed to feed my family. Thank you for that privilege.

Please forgive me, Father, for my previous grudging attitude. Help me remember mothers in other countries who are digging roots and searching for water. Help me relax and even enjoy this part of planning for my family. Help me choose healthy, whole foods, and make me aware more completely of just what You would have us eat. Let me be a welcome customer for the cashier to make her job a little more satisfying. Thank You, gracious God, for providing ample money, for I remember well the days it was difficult to make it stretch.

I saw a young mother appearing to struggle with her food stamps and said a quick, silent prayer for her situation. I tried to convey encouragement with a warm smile, for I felt at a loss just then as to what else to do for her. I wish I had thrown caution to the wind and bought her groceries for her that day. Later in my life, I did just that a couple of times, and it didn't ruin my budget one bit.

This brings to mind that there are food pantries for the homeless, and my home church always maintains a pantry for the needy. Help me to participate more in helping those who need it.

Thank You, Father for this revelation, in His name and always Your will be done, amen.

Embracing My Chores

But godliness with contentment is great gain.

—1 Timothy 6:6 (NIV)

"My Kitchen Prayer"

Bless my little kitchen, Lord
And light it with Thy love.
Help me plan and make my meals
From Thy heavenly home above.

Bless our meals with Thy presence
And warm them with Thy grace;
Watch over me as I do my work,
Washing pots and pans and plates.

The service I am trying to do
Is make my family content,
So bless my eager efforts, Lord,
and make them heaven sent.

When my young husband, our three little ones, and I made a major move away from all our family and lifetime friends, I quit my job and for the first time was a full-time wife and mother. The kitchen was the hub of our lives. For a while, it also felt like the drudge center of my days—preparing and serving meals, clearing up, washing and drying dishes (no dishwasher back then), wiping up splatters, taking out trash, and mopping the floor. And then doing it all over again two more times each day. *Arrrgghh!*

One day as I was shopping for a few small decorations for our new house, I ran across this kitchen prayer plaque. I know it was heaven sent; it jumped out at me, and I bought it on the spot (when usually then, every cent was carefully considered). I hung it over my kitchen stove where I saw it at least three times a day.

I began to pray about my aversion to the kitchen and the boredom I was feeling. Truthfully, I cannot tell you I immediately rejoiced over kitchen chores, but ultimately, I fell in love with cooking. The pleasure I found in relaxing while washing dishes in hot, soapy water and seeing shiny pretty dishes and then taking delight in a floor shining and free of ick soon helped me to not only accept but also be happy and content in my little kitchen. I prettied it up, and though I confess I was delighted when I did get help cleaning up, I grew to love that small room.

This little prayer on that plaque, too, had an effect on every aspect of housekeeping for me. I was no Pollyanna, believe me, but it did drastically forever change my attitude about making a comfortable nest for my family.

Many years later, our oldest daughter asked to take the little plaque to her new kitchen. I was so pleased. I had hopes she would find that little bit of comfort taken from the kitchen she had grown up in to sustain her during any trying times of her own.

Thank You, Father, for intervening when I needed it! Thank You for helping make me comfortable and happy in my role as wife, mother, and housekeeper. Bless those today who are trying to make comfortable places of retreat from the worlds for their own families, and give them respite when they need it. In the name of Jesus, Your will be done, amen.

Father's Day

The righteous (men) lead blameless lives; blessed are their children after them.

—Proverbs 20:7 (NIV)

So here it is, another blessed Lord's Day. In just a few days, it will be officially summer, and 'tis a soft day. All the spring thunderstorms have displayed their grandeur from time to time, and I am properly impressed. I am alone today, it is peacefully lovely, and I am mindful of praising you, Lord.

Father, I praise You that I am well enough to be alone. I am very much alone and quiet, yet I am full of thankfulness for it helps me focus on You. It is Father's Day. First, I am thankful for You, my heavenly Father. Thank You for deciding to put me here in Montana to finish out my full and rich life. Thank You for all my past escapes and for filling me with the Spirit enough to never forsake my faith even in the darkest darks. Thank You for keeping Your angels beside me as I edge ever closer to my forever home to be with You and my loved ones who have gone before me.

I thank You for the earthly father You chose for me, for his love and his faithfulness to all of us, but especially for his godliness, for his example, and for his teaching me about You. I thank You for my prince, who as head of our family as husband and father, fulfilled all that our children and I needed and more.

Thank You for allowing me to witness several fathers in my

family who were and are God-fearing, faithful leaders of their families. Father, I ask You for those whose fathers do not measure up and have let their families down to fill those children with Your love and mercy brimming over. Pour over them a joyous delight in You with tangible, special blessings that grant them hope for the future. And Father, touch those erring fathers so that they will be moved to return to their Creator.

And now, Father, as I worship You, I praise You for a myriad of blessings I cannot count. As I read Your Word and partake of the remembrance of Your Son's sacrifice, please bless me with a pure heart as I enter this communion. Strengthen and heal me enough to continue my life as You would have me live it for however long You have planned. Your will as always be done, in Jesus's blessed name, amen.

Goodbye Again

He will not leave you nor forsake you; do not fear nor be dismayed.

—Deuteronomy 31:8 (NKJV)

My prince worked out of town for twelve years; he would come home most weekends. Here is a sliver from my memory, a treasured loving memory.

He left this morning, bags packed, with both the excitement of his coming assignment and the regret of leaving etched on his face. Before he left, he took my hand and held it a moment, kissed my fingers, and then kissed my palm. When he looked up at me, he closed my hand around his kiss and said, "This is me kissing you till I get back."

Father, You know he isn't usually the most poetic kind of guy, but thank You for prompting this unforgettable moment between us, and I ask in the name of Jesus that You place Your strongest angels around him and bring him back to me. Shelter him, Father, under Your wings. In the name of Jesus, I ask You, amen.

And from the vantage point of old age many years later, thank You, Father, for always having brought him back to me. I surrendered him to You very reluctantly, but I am delighted that he

is free of pain and healthy and resting. He was a very hard worker, and I know he earned his new body. Thank You for Your angels around him all his life and for escorting him home to paradise. In Jesus's name, amen.

Heartbreak

*My flesh and my heart may fail, But God is the strength of
my heart and my portion forever.*

—*Psalm 73:26 (NIV)*

A friend's story as she told me follows.

"Let me go get the doctor."

The technician's face and its sudden concern stopped my heart,
and I sincerely regretted coming to this appointment alone. No, we
hadn't planned for this baby, and he just added to the three we already
had, but my love could not have been more intense for this little guy
at seven months' gestation.

**Father, I trust you to get me through this, for I have to be strong
for his daddy and three little excited siblings. Oh how will I tell
them?**

**Father God, I am stuffing my grief, but I'm longing to be in
my closet to collapse and howl out my sorrow. "Be thankful in
all things"—Baloney! You'll have to help me with thankfulness,
please, Father. Today, I am leveled. Forgive me, but I am weak,
and right now, the only thing I'm thankful for is knowing You'll
never leave me.**

So Father, after the fact, these many years later, that little one
is not forgotten. Please, Father, comfort all those who have lost
a child at any time of their lives and give them peace and blessed

memories. You know what it is to watch Your Son die. I thank You for Your compassion for those parents left behind.

For the unborn, we rejoice that You will gather us all, and You tell us we will know each other in heaven, and there will be no more tears there. I look forward to meeting our two little ones lost to us those many years ago. Thank You for three of my own children's safe deliveries and for my being able to enjoy their lives. Please give them long lives in Your service. In His name, Your will be done, amen.

Fragrances of My Life

For we are to God the pleasing aroma of Christ among those
who are being saved and those who are perishing.
—2 Corinthians 2:15 (NIV)

Do you have a favorite fragrance? I once thought I did, but then I remembered burying my face in Mama's freshly picked bunch of sweet peas, inhaling their pure sweetness, and thinking surely that that was my favorite.

Or Daddy handing me one of his red, ripe tomatoes, beautiful in its symmetry and color but distinctly and satisfyingly redolent with that clean, crisp, gardeny, tomatoey perfume that makes your mouth water.

When I was a teenager, my daddy planted night-blooming jasmine outside our bedroom windows. In the summer, drifting off to sleep in that rich jasmine warmth was unforgettable.

How about my babies, sound asleep and heavy on my shoulder with their fresh-from-the-angels baby's breath, honey-sweet against my neck?

How about the clean laundry scent from my beloved's T-shirt when I laid my head on his chest. An unforgettable essence remains as I remember inhaling the underlying deep, male, bath-soap scent of his warm skin as he wrapped his big arms about me.

Father God, how infinite are Your continuing blessings that enhance the beauty of this world. You have enriched the loveliness

of moments in time by bestowing these myriad of fragrances, sometimes subtly, sometimes blatantly flooding our senses.

Thank You, Father, for perfuming our days and nights with this heavenly touch from Your storehouse of surprises. Thank You that we have heaven ahead that holds all the glorious fragrances for us as a reward. In His holy name, amen.

Pearls from Mrs. Rembrandt

Besides "Jo," "Joey," "Sweets," "Love," and sometimes "Honey," my prince often called me "Mrs. Rembrandt." I am a painter—mostly oils and some acrylics—and of course he thought all my paintings were masterpieces; thus the name Mrs. Rembrandt.

Many years ago, a friend used to impart her pearls of wisdom to me from time to time and would say, "Let me give you a pearl." I hope to give you a few pearls today of my own.

In thinking of my delightful hours adding up to more than forty years of painting and the deep satisfaction and joy it brought me, I wondered why it had taken me so long to fulfill that yearning to express myself. I didn't begin painting until I was about forty. My older sister is an accomplished china artist whose work has been displayed for years in the World China Museum, and frankly, I was intimidated. I thought there was no way I could come up to her level of exquisite work and just didn't even try, never realizing it was not a competition. But that was one of my excuses back then.

That sister encouraged me to paint; she once even sent me money for supplies and asked me, "Now what's your excuse?" But the main reason I delayed was that I felt those hours of dedicating myself to creating would be taking away from my "real" job. I thought that somehow, my Christian walk should not include painting. But I've since learned better!

I am amazed at the number of people who tell me almost the same thing and won't give themselves time to devote to their passions. This is for those who haven't begun to drink from that deep well of talent God gave them and for the workaholics who won't slow down.

God Himself gave me the talent and the desire for color and design. My painting came shining through when I was finally ready and found dedicated teachers willing to share with me, teach me, and bring out what He had planted in me in the first place. It blossomed when I no longer felt I would be somehow cheating by having so much fun and relaxation. When I began to paint, I discovered that it didn't take away from my family and friends at all. To my amazement, it was only an enhancement!

I wanted desperately to paint all of God's amazing nature—its animals domesticated as well as the wonderfully wild, its spectacular sunrises, sunsets, turbulent oceans, and placid mountain lakes alike. I was especially drawn to His best creation, faces—portraits—and I really wanted to paint them and do justice to each one. Every face is different, and He fashioned each one with beauty, reflected happiness, and sometimes silent pain that nevertheless was written on the face. The record of events imprinted there among all the crevices and wrinkles tells the story of that person's unique life. I never knew I could be taught techniques that would allow me to fulfill my desire and capture those faces, but I soon learned through my treasured teachers that I could be taught. I could paint!

A dear painting friend taught me a treasured lesson one day during one of our conversations. She asked me if I ever prayed over my paintings. I told her that I did occasionally but in a willy-nilly sort of way. She said that before starting each of hers, she dedicated it to the Lord and asked His blessing as she painted. Oh my! Did that ever resonate with me, and it immediately became my habit too.

It had already long been my practice to write the scripture reference "Philippians 4:4–8 NIV" on the back of each of my paintings. I did not write out the words of the verses themselves on the painting, but here they are.

Rejoice in the Lord always. I will say it again: Rejoice!
Let your gentleness be evident to all. The Lord is near. Do

not be anxious about anything, but in every situation, by prayer and petition, with thanksgiving, present your requests to God. And the peace of God, which transcends all understanding, will guard your hearts and your minds in Christ Jesus. Finally, brothers and sisters, whatever is true, whatever is noble, whatever is right, whatever is pure, whatever is lovely, whatever is admirable—if anything is excellent or praiseworthy—think about such things.

It was such a joy to paint. I hoped that the recipients of every painting I gave away or sold would read those verses and receive some of the happiness I had enjoyed while painting it. My dream was fulfilled, and I loved every minute of it. I was silly about it in fact, for I loved the smell of turpentine and even loved cleaning my brushes. Many a time, I spent hours at my easel totally forgetting time, food, and troubles; I was entranced in another world of capturing that elusive something that made any one work enchanting.

My prince would come in to stop me for a break with a sandwich and a glass of water and make me get up and walk around a bit to get my blood circulating again. He'd say, "Come on, Mrs. Rembrandt, it's break time!" I had a dear friend who always went with me to painting workshops, and she would also remind me to stop to eat and drink and take a break, and I loved her for that.

You might ask me if I was successful, so here's my assessment of that. I was a smashing success as far as my own satisfaction, enjoyment, and relaxation were concerned. Part of that enjoyment was the kudos I received from my fans who to this day build me up and love everything I've painted. On the other hand, there were some who wouldn't give a plug nickel for my work and didn't mind letting me know it wasn't their "cup o' tae." A good lesson for me. I do wish I could have pleased a couple in my own family, but one way or another, it just wasn't that important to me.

Regardless, most of the folks in my family were my biggest fans. What was important was to keep the love going! Moneywise, I enjoyed a modicum of success and sold just enough to pay for most of my supplies. Part of the problem was that I gave away far more than I sold, but that was always been just fine with me.

If I can capture on canvas a moment in time or an expression on a wonderful face and then share what I've done with someone who appreciates and delights in it, is that not God's calling also? I know it is. And I call that success.

So that brings me to my pearls. What's stopping you from setting aside time to pursue your passion, perhaps your secret dream of maybe sculpting? Over and over, I hear, "But I have no talent! I was skipped over when it came to that!" Baloney! Here's a pearl or two, so listen up. Anyone who mows a lawn and carefully edges and smartens up the yard and loves doing it is expressing his or her talent. Maybe you plant flowers and stick them here and there and everywhere. That is adding beauty to the world; the talent of bringing beauty where there was none before is your gift!

Maybe you are a cake baker; your cakes are delicious and sought after by family and friends, and you are always asked to bring one of your cakes. What do you think that is? That's one of your gifts God gave you. Voila! You're creating!

I have a younger sister who consistently claims she has no talent. Let me tell you about her. She is a full-time dental assistant who takes special pride in helping the littlest patients with her dimples, smiles, and charming stories. Forgive me, sister, but she is a senior citizen way past retirement age. She has a smile that brightens the darkest days, and her soft hand patting your hand has a language all its own; it says, *I love you, I care about you, and I'm here for you.*

She bakes pies and cakes and makes cookies and casseroles that go to shut-ins, and she does it with a flair and energy. She might unexpectedly throw in a bag of Gummies or Hershey bites or M&Ms because, she says, "Life isn't life without a little candy once in a while."

She has a unique, whimsical handwriting that once you've seen it, it asks all by itself, *Isn't life wonderful?* That's how joyous her writing is, and she writes loving, encouraging notes that make you laugh just seeing the envelope. Laughing is her specialty, but if you need a shoulder, need someone to cry with you, look her up. You'll never find more compassion or understanding. And she says she has no talent!

What about auto mechanics who delve into the mysteries of transmissions and spark plugs and those Star Wars computers in autos? Those guys are wizards. They take your dead car, bring it to life, and return it to you sometimes vacuumed and with shined-up windows, a wash, and a wax job to boot. So what if they can't paint? Fixing cars requires talent, and how grateful I am they can do it. I couldn't fix my car if my life depended on it, but it's their gift.

There are heroes and there are heroes; plumbers are right up there among them. Who doesn't admire and respect their plumbers if they have a good one? I always poured mine a cup of coffee and asked if he needed ice water. I was always relieved when I heard, "All fixed. You can run your water now." Can you figure out the vagaries of the dark world of pipes and valves and icky water? Not me. That takes not only talent but also dedication and the willingness to get dirty and work on your knees all hunched over half your life.

I thought of plumbers because I once apologized to my plumber for his having to work in the cold and with his big smile he said, something like, *I love what I do! Nothing more satisfying to me than putting a broken-down system back together and knowing another home is running smoothly.* I was amazed. Here was a happy man utilizing to the fullest his gift and acknowledging his talent.

So maybe none of that is you and you'd rather swing a golf club, a tennis racket, go fishing, or sit treading a spinning wheel learning that old-world craft of spinning yarn. Do you see that God put different gifts in different people but that sometimes you don't recognize what He gave you is truly a gift? Don't sell yourself short no matter what.

I know that many of you are already deeply entrenched in satisfying hobbies. But if you aren't, I give you my permission to go buy that sketchbook and set of pencils. Sign up for ceramics. Go join the community choir, sing your heart out, and love every minute of it. Get yourself some videos and learn how to make jewelry, or pot plants, or build a doghouse. Perhaps you don't want a solitary pastime. Okay, so take a wonderful book or two and go read to the elderly. So many are losing or have already lost their eyesight. Go to youth clubs in your town and volunteer to teach the kids there to bake cookies or how to sink a basketball.

Whatever is deep inside, go for it. The point is that you should not bury the talent God has given you. The peace that envelops your being after your pleasurable hour or two or three of developing that talent or engaging in it is priceless. Our medical people tell us our endorphins rise measurably! The pearl in this is for you to allow time to let the dust settle; take the time to reflect on the blue horizon and a lone sailboat while you wriggle your toes in the sand.

A fact of life about daily living is work, and we are all very familiar with that. What some of us tend to forget is that God rested on the seventh day, and in the Old Testament, He commanded His people to rest. Even Jesus in His ministry withdrew from crowds to renew and refresh Himself. Nowadays, it's more usual than not to run to worship services, get them over with, and then rush to accomplish whatever the weekend was reserved for. The pearl in this is to slow down and remember, "Be still and know that I am God" (Psalm 46:10 NIV). Find some uninterrupted time to develop your gifts. Carve out time for an appointment with yourself, and write it on your calendar if need be.

God made these creative and different desires in each of us. Please understand the point—we don't all have to be poets or painters or anything we usually think of as artistic to be artists in our own right. Give back to yourself what God gave you in the first place, and let those talents rise and delight you. You may just be a better person for it!

Father, in the name of Jesus, Your generous gifts of our different talents make our lives so much richer. Thank You for those times we can immerse ourselves in the delight of creativity, and help us always to do it for Your glory. Help those of us who don't even realize our potential to bring it to full flower by providing a way for us to fulfill it. Thank You for the diversity in this world You created for us, and thank You for the beauty and the function in it. Your will always, amen.

Autumn

Autumn is a lovely, slowing-down time of the year that brings mellowing fall colors and cooling to the land. Then about the time you get all your summer clothes put away, here comes a blast of summer heat. The air is fragrant with hints of smoke and the crisp, pungent smell of mounds of drifting red, yellow, maroon, and brown leaves piling up. Geese call out their promise to be back as they fly beautiful formations south. There's an expectation in the air, one of coming cool days, cold nights, and warm fires for snuggling-in family nights. Holidays and all the family gatherings and children laughing are just around the corner.

In the autumn of my life, I enjoyed a slowing and a calming that was so satisfying. Yet, at the same time, some of the darkest times of my life blasted me. Marriages and grandchildren changed the entire makeup of my little family, and my cherished holiday traditions changed out of necessity. I experienced some of my highest highs and then some of my lowest lows. As always, God's gentle mercy sustained me, and reward of friends and family, my ever-uplifting sisters, loving nieces and nephews, rambunctious, precious grandchildren, and eventually my beloved great-grandkids lit up our lives, and that light is still glowing.

Draw Me Nearer

Make me know Your ways, O LORD; Teach me Your paths.
Lead me in Your truth and teach me, For You are the God of
my salvation; For You I wait all the day.
—Psalm 25:4–5 (NIV)

As a child, I had an impression in my mind of God as Leonardo da Vinci's painting on the Sistine Chapel ceiling, which depicts him reaching out to touch Adam to fill him with life. I was awestruck, fearful, and totally intimidated by God's muscles, power, and white hair and beard. As I matured in my spiritual walk, I had no clear vision of Him—just a nebulous omnipotence in my mind.

One quiet afternoon much later in life, I was resting in my recliner praying when I suddenly realized that for some time, I had been picturing Father God again as a personage. Though details of His appearance were unclear and almost misty, I definitely imagined Him as sitting on the couch opposite me listening for all He was worth. He seemed to be my kind Father who was relaxed and wanted to hear what I had to say. I was thrilled with the feeling of my heavenly Father sitting comfortably in my family room with me and absolutely cherished those moments. There were no contours and details in that vision, just a feeling of the sacred trust of a quiet afternoon visit. The feeling of closeness is hard to describe, but I felt whole, nourished, and loved.

I suspect that has happened to you too. I have periods of extreme closeness and an intense desire to read the Word, pray, draw every bit of spiritual knowledge I can glean from my walk with Him, and bask in the presence of my Lord and Savior. Our visit in my family room that day felt so naturally right and so supernaturally awesome.

Other times, it seems I struggle, and I am in a sort of mundane, almost blasé mind-set, and it takes either determination to deliberately pull myself out of it or, sadly, an emergency situation that is out of my control, and then I'm frightened right back to His throne. Those dry, desert times feel dangerous. I think the only solution is immersing myself in the many scriptures that ask the Father to teach us to know Him better and to draw closer to Him. I share a few here.

> Teach me to do Your will, For You are my God; Let Your good Spirit lead me on level ground. (Psalm 143:10 NIV)

> But if any of you lacks wisdom, let him ask of God, who gives to all generously and without reproach, and it will be given to him. (James 1:5 NIV)

> Let me hear Your loving kindness in the morning; For I trust in You; Teach me the way in which I should walk; For to You I lift up my soul. (Psalm 143:8 NIV)

> O send out Your light and Your truth, let them lead me; Let them bring me to Your holy hill And to Your dwelling places. (Psalm 43:3 NIV)

> Trust in the LORD with all your heart And do not lean on your own understanding. In all your ways acknowledge Him, And He will make your paths straight. (Proverbs 3:5–6 NIV)

> Search me, O God, and know my heart; Try me and know my anxious thoughts; And see if there be any hurtful way in me, And lead me in the everlasting way. (Psalm 139:23–24 NIV)

> I will instruct you and teach you in the way which you should go; I will counsel you with My eye upon you. Do not

be as the horse or as the mule which have no understanding, Whose trappings include bit and bridle to hold them in check, Otherwise they will not come near to you. (Psalm 32:8–9 NIV)

Call to me and I will answer you and tell you great and unsearchable things you do not know. (Jeremiah 33:3 NIV)

"Draw Me Nearer" is an old hymn I love. You might remember singing it in services. The words speak volumes of what is in my own heart.

I am Thine, O Lord, I have heard Thy voice,
And it told Thy love to me;
But I long to rise in the arms of faith
And be closer drawn to Thee.

(Refrain)
Draw me nearer, nearer blessed Lord,
To the cross where Thou hast died;
Draw me nearer, nearer, nearer blessed Lord,
To Thy precious, bleeding side.

Consecrate me now to Thy service, Lord,
By the pow'r of grace divine;
Let my soul look up with a steadfast hope,
And my will be lost in Thine.

Oh, the pure delight of a single hour
That before Thy throne I spend,
When I kneel in prayer, and with Thee, my God
I commune as friend with friend!

There are depths of love that I cannot know
Till I cross the narrow sea;
There are heights of joy that I may not reach
Till I rest in peace with Thee.

So, my heavenly Father, thank You for the closeness that has happened as I've grown older. My desire to know You better only increases. I'm asking You to take Psalm 139:23–24 and consider these verses as part of my prayer to increase my knowledge and appreciation of You and Your world and "lead me in the everlasting Way."

As my days shorten here, help me to know confidently where I'm going and with delight enter the place You've prepared for me. Today, You know the readers and what they need and where they are in the knowledge of Your will. Place the desire and the ability in all of us to absorb exactly what You want us to know, and as we learn, let us share the good news as we know it with the world. In His name, Your will always be done, amen.

Single-Minded

Now to the unmarried and the widows I say: It is good for them to stay unmarried, as I do.

—*1 Corinthians 7:8 (NIV)*

I have been privileged to have the most precious friend who was single until she was forty. She drove a couple of hours to visit me in the hospital after I had back surgery many years ago, and she spent the afternoon with me. How honored I was that during her visit, she shared her story. She told me that although she desperately wanted marriage and family and though she had several chances, she couldn't bring herself to marriage because each time she was stopped in her spirit and unable to commit.

As a Christian, she never ceased praying. This woman was and still is a beauty, physically and spiritually. Soft, sweet words, but so fun-loving and feisty too. Smart as a whip and loving. She finally decided God's plan did not include marriage, so for twenty of her adult years, she dedicated herself to living for Him, and she did. She filled her life with her career, and after work, she spent hours in His service.

Finally, at age forty, she met the love of her life, a widower and doctor with four teenagers who fell for her too. She said she always had faith in God but had decided that He wanted her single. Well, in a lovely late surprise, He brought her a Christian husband and a ready-made family. They did have one child of their own, and their life together was more than what she had prayed for all those years.

He is now in heaven, and today, she's in her nineties, but she is surrounded by children, grandchildren and great-grandchildren, a living example of faithfulness and hope fulfilled.

My Aunt Lillian and Uncle Clarence were childless. When I was fifteen and visiting their farm, I asked her how she felt about not having children. Her reply astonished me. "No children? Honey, God gave me hundreds of children! I've been teaching Sunday school for so long that my first students are now bringing their little ones, and I'm teaching them!"

Aunt Lil went on to say that yes, she wanted children when she was young, but when she discovered it was not to be, she realized that when the other teachers complained about not having time enough to prepare lessons that she had plenty of time. I remember her and my Gramma Sullivan, who lived with her then, preparing visual aids for lessons and gifts for her students to take home on special days. She thought up prizes for memory work, and took homemade cookies and farm-fresh milk for snacks. Gramma and Aunt Lil were both handy with the crochet hooks, and they crocheted small items for birthdays.

She said she regularly had grown men who towered over her come see her through the years (one even swung her around) and tell her how much her classes had meant to them. She said the little daughters of some of the girls she had taught years before sometimes asked her if their mamas said their "memory work" "as good as I can".

Aunt Lil found her children in teaching, and she told me that she was rewarded every day, especially every time a former student thanked her. But what about other childless wives or widows, widowers, divorced, and the never married? What of their loneliness? There are countless unmarried who are not lonely and live their lives out in contentment. Paul himself advised staying unmarried to be able to completely commit to serving the Lord without distraction.

But for some of you, those who are single either by choice or chance, the reality of being alone day after day, night after night, year after year may become daunting. First things first. Seek God's plan in prayer for yourself, and listen and watch for His direction and opportunities. Consider this—you are much more free than married people are to decide everything for yourself, what you want to do, and where you want to serve. Don't be just a lonely little petunia in an onion patch; look for areas in which you can use your expertise and do what you enjoy. If you assess your talents and see where your specialty can fit into His way, you will find a place where you can be a big help. Be faithful in attendance to worship, treasure your friendships, and listen for opportunities to help. Meanwhile, revel in the fact that if you want to eat a pint of Häagen-Dazs ice cream for dinner once in a while, there is no one there to scold you!

Just because you're alone doesn't mean you can't host or help out on wiener or hamburger cookouts for the youth or volunteer to drive on excursions to the roller rink or for ice skating. If you aren't a teacher, are you a cook? Can you help set up and break down during fellowship? Take a look at the churchyard. Can it use some TLC, and is gardening your "cup o' tae"? Do the pews need polishing?

Do you have a heart for the elderly? If so, you can collect the list of shut-ins and take them appropriate snacks and sit and read to one of them for a half hour or just visit with them—they truly are often very lonely. Hold their hands while you are there, for human touch is something they long to feel again. Volunteer at the hospital, at the public library, at the museum—or not. Getting out in your community will give you chances to meet new people and increase your opportunities to gently share the Lord with them. Find the place you fit. Finding your niche, even a very small niche, will greatly enrich your life.

Are you an athlete? I have an unmarried friend who is still athletic and if not in her seventies yet, she's getting close. She's still lovely, smart as a whip, and yes, she had a yen for her own family, but she always felt a stop to the opportunities that came. So she dedicated herself to young people with tennis games or golf games with hamburgers afterward. Several of these young people had one or more parents missing or gone on temporary duty in the military. She has given substantial service during her lifetime, and she is well respected, actually much loved, and has a host of friends. Many seek out her precious smile and hearty encouragements repeatedly. My son benefited greatly from this dear one's attention while his father was working away from home, and she is well remembered in my family as someone forever young and forever laughing.

Expand your family from within your brothers and sisters in the Lord, and surround yourself with like-minded people. Friends are often closer than family. Paul addressed the Corinthians about married and unmarried people.

> I would like you to be free from concern. An unmarried man is concerned about the Lord's affairs—how he can please the Lord. But a married man is concerned about the affairs of this world—how he can please his wife—and his interests are divided. An unmarried woman or virgin is concerned about the Lord's affairs: Her aim is to be devoted to the Lord in both body and spirit. But a married woman is concerned about the affairs of this world—how she can please her husband. I am saying this for your own good, not to restrict you, but that you may live in a right way in undivided devotion to the Lord. (1 Corinthians 13:32–35 NIV)

As a single, you will endure occasional loneliness; that's part of it. But there is this. Your single life spares you from the pain of interaction with the woes of a partner and all that entails. "For better for worse, in sickness and in health" is part of the nitty-gritty of marriage. The pain of watching your beloved suffering from work-related problems, injuries, illnesses, or financial setbacks takes tough-mindedness, willingness to acquiesce at appropriate times, and resilience. I felt it was worth it, but I surely would understand those who would rather skip it.

If you will indulge me a few moments, here are a few more words of advice from a gramma who has lived mostly alone the last seven years. If this turns you off, skip it by all means, but I'm offering it as a reminder, just a little nudge to keep yourself perking along. When you are alone, I know how easy it is to neglect yourself. If I didn't have a daughter regularly checking on me, I know I'd fail to do some of the urgent things that keep me healthy.

So see to it you have regular healthy meals that keep your weight steady. Don't neglect plenty of proteins, fresh veggies and fruits, and not too many starches. One of my quick, easy, and yummy snacks or even meals is a smoothie made of one cup of cottage cheese, a half cup of cut-up cantaloupe, and a half cup of pineapple—fresh or canned— whipped in a blender. There's protein and good carbohydrates full of fiber. I like to sweeten mine with just a half teaspoon of agave. It might take a quarter of a cup of water, more or less, to keep it from being too thick. You can make a myriad of combinations for smoothies, but this is a quick and delicious pick-me-up. Exercise regularly, whatever it takes to move your body, something you enjoy so you'll actually do it. Check on vitamins and supplements with your doctor, and don't fail your teeth or miss dental appointments.

You may or may not be a workaholic, but either way, get away from your job and make time for something you look forward to every night after work—a good book, a movie, working in your rose garden, or dinner with a friend. Whatever it is, keep up a recreational schedule so that you are fulfilled and find it a pleasure to come into your own home and climb into your own comfortable bed at night. When you have had your last conversation with Father God, close your eyes and let the angels sing you to sleep!

Father God, as always, I am asking a favor, and now I pray for people who are alone, especially the lonely. Father, show them their paths to productive and happy living, show them laughter and joy, let them feel Your love, and keep them ever under Your wings. In Jesus's name, amen.

The Slow Movement

He says, "Be still, and know that I am God; I will be exalted among the nations, I will be exalted in the earth."
—Psalm 46:10 (NIV)

This morning on a quilting show I like to watch, the gentleman teaching it mentioned the "slow movement." He said it was simply slowing down life's pace and giving ourselves time to fully live in the moment. According to him, it is catching on nationally across all areas of people's lives. I haven't seen evidence of that yet, but he said he had been on "fast" for years.

Over the past twenty years, he taught and made numerous quilts as quickly as he could for classes and workshops but never stopped long enough to make himself a quilt. He decided to do just that by employing "slow." He found himself concentrating on just the task at hand instead of worrying about what was for dinner or paying bills. His calm approach benefited him in ways he hadn't thought about before, and it was carrying over into the rest of his life.

He said he actually did not move slower; in fact, he sewed very fast. He just narrowed his thinking to the enjoyment of the one thing he was working on. He listened to the rhythmic sound of the purring sewing machine and inhaled the fragrance of the freshly ironed fabrics. He really looked at and enjoyed the pleasurable patterns and colors with which he was working. He said that during this relaxed approach to quilting, he found himself praying, and that intrigued me.

This slowing down is something I've been trying for the past twenty years or so. It is the antithesis of all I'd learned as a young woman. My daughter called me the original multitasker because I used shortcuts, rushed around, and filled every moment of every day with as much as I could possibly cram in it.

I remember the thrill of my first microwave because of the time it saved, and today, having very little stamina, I still consider it a godsend. In literally less than a minute, I have bacon hot and crisp for my breakfast even if the fragrance isn't as rich. I remember getting out the old black-iron skillet, prying the cold pieces of bacon from their package fresh from the fridge, and slapping those slices one by one onto the hot pan. I can hear the *pssssshhhh* and the comforting pops and sizzles and crackles sputtering away. I again smell the full, hot, bacony flavor wafting up from the pan and the bread toasting. I watch for perfect doneness in the beautiful yellow orbs of sizzling sunny-side-up eggs. Quickly enough, there was a lovely and tasty breakfast for my family. I found something very satisfying in the sound and smell and taste of such slow cooking that is surely lost in microwaving.

I'm thinking of Jesus and His apostles walking everywhere in their sandals on those hot, dusty roads and out of necessity having to rest under whatever shade they could find. They got there when they got there. I know the Bible teaches us against sloth and waste, but somehow, I think that in the past, I have overscheduled and overdone some things. I think I will like this "slow movement," and I'm pretty sure our Father approves too.

> *This is what the Sovereign Lord, the Holy One of Israel, says:*
> *"In repentance and rest is your salvation, in quietness and*
> *trust is your strength." (Isaiah 30:15 NIV)*

Father God, in His name, grant us the wisdom to choose balance in our lives, to choose You as our priority. Bless our families with quiet times together feeding each other's needs and slowing down to truly smell the roses. Your will always be done, amen.

In His Light

But if we walk in the light, as he is in the light, we have fellowship with one another, and the blood of Jesus, his Son, purifies us from all sin.

—1 John 1:7 (NIV)

Have you ever been in a totally dark place? I understand that there are caves where they turn out the lights, and the dark is different from what we are used to. I remember once experiencing a dark so dark that I became disoriented. It was an oppressive and seemingly palpable dark that pushed against my face and body. Someone lit a candle, and that warm, pulsating, little glow of warmth felt like life itself had just reappeared. I felt safe again.

Only in the darkness do we perceive the star shining. Only at the deep hour of midnight, when vision is dim and we stumble to find our way, are we able to completely appreciate the freedom light brings. Only in the gloom of despair is the bright glimmer of hope to light our path so deeply anticipated and appreciated.

For now we see through a glass, darkly, but then face to face: now I know in part; but then shall I know even as also I am known. (1 Corinthians 13:12 KJV)

Are you feeling darkness? Seek the light. Be the light. Our Father has given us an unquenchable desire and ability for brightness, so we should look to the light of His love. Delving into His Word invariably brings the light of hope and the promise of safety in Him. Surround yourself with people whose inner light shines so brightly that it reflects on you. However, realize He has given you all you need to nurture even a tiny flame of faith and bring into the full brilliance the crackling fire of trust and confidence to step into His light forever.

Thank You, Father, for the times of darkness because only in the contrast of that blackness against star shine and daylight can we fully appreciate the true beauty of His shining. In His name, Your will be done, amen.

A Lord's Day in Autumn

But seek first the kingdom of God and His righteousness,
and all these things shall be added to you. Therefore do not
worry about tomorrow, for tomorrow will worry about its
own things.

—Matthew 6:33–34 (NIV)

Again, it is the Lord's Day. Something special always settles on me on Sunday. It's as if all nature knows it's His day, and somehow I think I would recognize it even without a calendar.

Today, autumn is in the air. At night, my nose is nipped as I stick my head out to check out the stars. There is a subtle change in the quality of light; the smell on the breeze predicts change, and I fill my lungs with autumn air that feels fresher, different, almost tingling.

This quiet morning as I sip my coffee, I watch and listen to an encouraging preacher on TV. He reminds me that when I am in deep water, He is right there with me—big storms, bigger God.

I turn off the TV and just listen to the wind, for the breeze is gusting, and I watch two geese in the air struggling a bit against the blow. Soon, they will all fly south, and the sky will seem emptier without their lovely flocks flying in formation. Though autumn is my favorite season, a melancholy hits that speaks of treasured times past, the cooling down of summer, and loved ones and little ones grown and gone.

As if to lessen the loss, there is a new brilliance in the changing leaves that electrifies whole forests—a visual delight. The scent of smoke in the air reminds us of hearth and warmth and home, and soon, many homecomings will refresh our spirits during the coming holidays. The nostalgia of memories that brings tears as well as smiles is tempered with His mercies ever renewing. The promise of seasons to come lies deep in the sleeping seeds and in joyous announcements of expected new babies!

Yes, seasons change, but He is the same always. He is with me now and always as He was with my parents and grandparents, walking every step with them as He does with me now, guiding our families into the future. It is a mystery to me how He is with me here now and yet He is there with you right now as you read, and yet even more in heaven preparing greater rewards for us than we can imagine.

This Lord's Day, this privileged time of praise and worship, I hear the gusting winds blow and the old wind chimes clanging in the cool, crystal air. A collection of dry leaves hurries along, quietly skittering and rustling along the deck.

I thank You, Father, once again, for the treasure of today and the unequaled peace of the Lord's Day.

A Second Cup of Coffee

Oh give thanks to the LORD, for He is good, For His loving kindness is everlasting.

—*Psalm 107:1 (NIV)*

Coffee didn't do it for me this morning, nor have two Excedrin, and I haven't brushed my teeth. It will be one of those slog-through-the-mud days. *Where is my joy? And what happened to my energy?* I sullenly start the dishwasher and lean forward to raise the shade.

It is quiet, and the lavender light hasn't given way to the sun yet, when suddenly a big ray of yellow slides over the hill lighting a brilliant path across the lawn. I stand transfixed by the sight of bright-yellow, little dandelions beaming their hellos at me. Their sparkling diamonds of dew are twinkling a *Cheer up!* across the green grass. I laugh, splash cold water in my face, and breathe a heartfelt "Thank you."

I eye my still fresh pot of coffee, glance out once again at the lovely scene through the window, and reach for my favorite mug.

A Friendship Closed

Even my close friend Even I trusted, Who ate my bread, Has lifted up his heel against me. But You, O LORD, be gracious to me and raise me up.

—Psalm 41:9–10 (NIV)

I had a dear friend to whom something happened. I know it was another dart from Satan, but my reaction was this.

She's my friend, Father God. What do I do? What did I do to deserve her cutting me off? Haven't I been a good friend to her, and haven't I even sacrificed for her? I've taken time away from my family for her and sometimes wore myself out for her. What's the deal?

So Father, in the name of Jesus, forgive me for my part in this painful time, and give me clarity in how to proceed with my friend, whom I love. Be with her, Father, too, and heal anything that would keep us in disharmony. If our season together is over and this should end, keep my mouth shut and let only love come through when I speak of her. Your will be done always, in Jesus's name, amen.

Understanding never came, and the old relationship never resumed, but God gave me peace and only love for her, and the pain of it is gone.

Thank You, Father.

What? No Santa Claus?

And you will know the truth, and the truth will set you free.
—John 8:32 (NIV)

I was in second grade, a time in my young life when fairies, elves, and Santa Claus and his reindeer flourished. Yes, I was taught about God and his precepts, but there was my separate entrenched belief in fantasy. That day at school, a classmate declared there was actually no Santa Claus! Earth shattering.

Our rental home then had a little flowerbed where Daddy planted colorful fuchsias and baby's tears moss. The moss provided a small, tender, emerald-green carpet for me to play ballerina fairies. I turned the delicate fuchsia blossoms upside down, twirled them around, and voila! There were graceful little fairy ballerinas in their tutus.

That sad, disillusioned day, I sat cross-legged in front of that little flower bed and cried a lot declaring furiously that though Santa may not be, I knew for a fact fairies lived in that lovely fuchsia and moss-filled little bower. Hadn't I fancied I almost glimpsed them … almost? In a world of hurt, I finally accepted the truth.

Which brings me to raising my own children; I happily promoted all those beloved fantasies into their young lives. When one of my daughters was told by her friend about no Santa, my child was absolutely ruined so much that I remembered my own pain when I first learned that and began to rethink the matter. How did I justify teaching Santa and fairies with my very real God, Jesus, and the Holy Spirit?

I remember the look on her face when she said, "Mama, you lied to me!" Oh, the worst pain—I had wounded my beloved child. I decided that if I had it to do over and from then on, for our family, I'd make it clear from the beginning that fantasy land was just that—a pretend world of fun make-believe

I still love the idea of the beauty and fun of fantasy, but I'm convinced children need to know exactly what fantasy is. First, our priority is to teach daily living in and for Him, not that Santa is watching to see whether we are naughty or nice.

My children raised my grandchildren without Santa and fairies and such. I admit that though I held my peace, nostalgic regret niggled at me, and I felt sorry for what they missed. However, those children today are calm, intelligent, happy, productive adults with no carryover weight of pretense by parents.

Father God, thank You for the beauty You created that does not need embellishment. Help us all to always speak truth to our little ones and establish in them the very real faith and trust in only You. Guide each family in their decision to include Santa or not, and help them find a way that is cohesive with Your will. Always only Your will be done. In His name, amen.

Angels around Us

The LORD has established His throne in heaven, and His kingdom rules over all. Praise the LORD, you His angels, you mighty ones who do His bidding, who obey His word. Praise the LORD, all His heavenly hosts, you His servants who do His will. Praise the LORD, all His works. Everywhere in His dominion. Praise the LORD, my soul.

—*Psalm 103:19–22 (NIV)*

So what have I learned over the years in my rather long but not truly in-depth study of angels? One major thing I was surprised to learn was that the Bible never mentions one specific angel assigned to each of us as our guardian angel. That was quite a disappointment until the further I read, I more I realized there are multiple angels assigned for each of us! How smart is that? Think about it. How many of us know people who would need more than one to get them out of the pickles they get themselves into?

There are warrior angels, praise-singing angels, messenger angels, and rescue angels. How I've longed to see one though I often say I've seen many precious friends or family who were earth angels in my estimation. Some paintings portray incredibly beautiful angels. My favorite old artist, whose gorgeous angels and Madonnas with baby are breathtakingly beautiful, is William Adolph Bouguereau. He was a French painter of the 1800s and early 1900s. I love every photo of his paintings I've seen. He worked in oil, and his genre was realism. I would love to think angels looked just as how he had painted them, but I can't find biblical descriptions that include wings and halos (except for the winged creatures mentioned in Revelation). I suspect angels are super beings who look like us but much prettier, handsomer, bigger, and stronger and with the air of superior serenity God gave them.

Gabriel is the angel most of us probably remember best for he is the one who gave Mary the good news of her coming son, Jesus. But Gabriel also announced the pregnancy of Elizabeth to Zachariah and that in their old age they would be parents to John the Baptist, who would spread the news far and wide that Jesus was coming.

In the Old Testament, Gabriel interpreted Daniel's prophetic vision of the end times. Each time he is mentioned, Gabriel was either met with fear or tries to quell the fears of those to whom he appeared. So I wondered what made him so fearful looking? Indeed, Daniel fell on his face when he saw him and was exhausted for days after their encounter and his vision. As he wrote in Daniel 8:17 (NIV), "As he came near the place where I was standing, I was terrified and fell prostrate."

Michael is a warrior angel, an archangel with authority over other angels. He is described in Daniel 10:13–21, Jude 1:9, and Revelation 12:7 as contending, fighting, or standing against evil spirits and principalities. Very little is said about him, but obviously, he is very powerful for he was described to Daniel as the protector of Israel. In Revelation, he is described as fighting along with other angels against "the dragon." He is in obedience and complete submission to the Lord. I noted with interest that in looking up references to Michael, I found a question-and-answer site that contained the statement, "Taking into consideration the strength of Michael the archangel, his submission to God is all the more beautiful."

While there are no consistent references to what angels usually wear, there are several scriptures that refer to angels' dazzling robes or their shining appearance, and the thousands of angels in Revelation are described as dressed in white linen.

The clothes of the angels who were seen at Christ's tomb were dazzling.

There was a violent earthquake, for an angel of the Lord came down from heaven and, going to the tomb, rolled back the stone and sat on it. His appearance was like lightning, and his clothes were white as snow. (Matthew 23:2–3 NIV)

And later, when the women went with spices to anoint Jesus's body,

They found the stone rolled away from the tomb, but when they entered, they did not find the body of the Lord Jesus. While they were wondering about this, suddenly two men in clothes that gleamed like lightning stood beside them. In their fright the women bowed down with their faces to the ground, but the men said to them, "Why do you look for the living among the dead? He is not here; he has risen!" (Luke 24:2–6 NIV)

But when three angels visited Abram to announce that Sarai would have a baby, they were described as three men, and no special dress was mentioned. In Joshua, though the angel's name was not mentioned, he was a warrior angel, the captain of the Lord's hosts who stood with sword drawn. He was obviously dressed as a soldier; Joshua approached him and asked, "Are you for us or against us?" That's when he instructed Joshua to take off his sandals because he was standing on holy ground.

I suspect that if one appeared here in Montana, he might have on jeans, cowboy hat, and boots and probably would be casually leaning against a pickup truck until he got what he had come for. I think they wear what they need to so they can fit into our world to move around as the situation warrants, right?

There are many scriptures about angels, but I love to envision angels rejoicing when a sinner repents.

In the same way, I tell you, there is rejoicing in the presence of the angels of God over one sinner who repents. (Luke 15:10 NIV)

I can picture the host of heaven in clusters laughing, chattering, and clapping their hands for joy so happy and grateful for the redemption of one more of God's children.

In Hebrews 1:14 (NIV), the scriptures describe one of the angel's jobs.

> *Are they not all ministering spirits, sent out to render service*
> *for the sake of those who will inherit salvation?*

It is also such a comfort to me to know that angels accompany us to our heavenly rest; Jesus spoke of that in the parable of the rich man and Lazarus. After Lazarus died, this is what He said.

> *The time came when the beggar died and the angels carried*
> *him to Abraham's side. Luke 16:22 (NIV)*

Revelation 5:11–12 (NIV) speaks of John's vision about the end of the ages; it is a powerful, lovely, and amazing peek into God's heavenly world.

> *Then I looked, and I heard the voice of many angels around*
> *the throne and the living creatures and the elders; and the*
> *number of them was myriads of myriads, and thousands of*
> *thousands, saying with a loud voice, "Worthy is the Lamb*
> *that was slain to receive power and riches and wisdom and*
> *might and honor and glory and blessing."*

There are many more wonderful stories about angel encounters, but I follow with just recording people and events I know about personally. A lovely family, longtime members of our church, told of a special event that had happened just minutes before the passing of the husband and father. Just before he died, he very calmly and quietly said, "Oh, here they are! The angels are here to take me." And they did just that—they took him home. I think this could be counted as witnessing a close encounter of the third kind and find it incredibly comforting.

I do know another very credible witness to an angelic visit here on earth not long ago. I'm telling her story with her permission though she is quite aware some may view it rather dubiously. Since my sister's husband died, she has lived alone and she is, like me, a senior saint.

One night, she was suddenly awakened and was immediately aware she was not alone. It was terrifying to her at first especially when she realized that she was not dreaming but was wide awake. Across the room were the shapes of two men, one very tall and one of medium height, standing side by side quietly watching her. She was so frightened that she pulled her covers over her head and prayed for the Father to protect her. Feeling more reassured, she was able to get up and go to the bathroom. They were still there when she returned, and again, she asked the Father's help to relax and get back to sleep. Interestingly, she did not try to talk to or question them, and they didn't speak either. But with the reassurance of the Lord, she was able to accept their presence and settle in for a good night's sleep.

Two more nights they appeared, just standing quietly, and her apprehension lessened each time. On the last night, they approached her bed not in a threatening way. One stood back while the other silently leaned over her. Was he saying, *Good night, sleep tight. We're leaving now?* They did indeed leave.

She and I talked about this, and we decided that for reasons unknown to her, Father God knew she needed reassurance that she was being watched over. Perhaps she did need more protection those particular nights, and He wanted her to be aware that protection was there for her. I find this event fascinating especially knowing my very down-to-earth sister who is not given to fits of fancy in the least. I'm wondering if I could have calmed down so well.

I had a lifelong friend from childhood whom I met in church when her father came to preach for us and brought his family. We all became friends, and her mother and mine dearly loved each other.

Many years later, my friend's mother was in the hospital dying of a brain tumor that was so large that she had to have part of her skull removed. That precious family endured weeks of tragedy and sadness during her hospitalization, and she was unable to open her eyes or talk for quite a while before the end.

Just minutes before she died, my friend told me her mother suddenly opened her eyes and pointed to the ceiling saying very clearly, "Look! It's so beautiful!" It was such an amazing event; my friend said she was stunned but very grateful that her mother had seen something beautiful. Was she seeing a vision of the beautiful gates of heaven? We know it is recorded in our Bible that angels escort us to our place of rest, and it's comforting to me to think she was seeing the beautiful angels who had come to take her most lovingly and compassionately to her heavenly home.

My husband and I became close and loving friends with a couple in church almost fifty-five years ago. The last year or so of the husband's life was spent in and out of the hospital, and his health was extremely precarious; it was a very trying time for them.

During one particularly difficult hospitalization, it became so wearing for him to be closed up in his room, hooked up to lines and machines with constant interruptions, close calls, and a very cranky, irritable heart. Our friend, his wife, decided a trip outside for fresh air and a break from cabin fever was just what he needed, and with the nurses' consent and help, she wheeled him, tubes, lines, oxygen, and all, out under a tree and into the beautiful air of that gentle afternoon. She described a lovely, well-dressed black man who stopped and exchanged pleasantries before he went in to visit someone inside.

Maybe twenty minutes later, he stopped and visited more with them, and they were surprised that this stranger knew many friends at their church because they had never seen him before. They felt an inexplicable camaraderie, and he told them things they did not know such as about several at church who had cancer, and he said he was praying for them. (Months later, my friends found out that yes, these church friends did indeed have cancer.) Seeing that my friend was obviously ill, the man asked if he could pray for him right then, and our friends were willing and happy to do that. That's when the fun began!

They joined hands, and as this man touched them, there was a feeling almost like an electric shock that passed through both of their bodies, and they were instantly filled with peace and an inexplicable calm so much so that the wife later told me she felt goose bumps. He prayed for our friend's health, but he prayed also for those at their church. She tried to describe the feeling she had never before experienced: "soul satisfying and indescribable," she called it—a lifting, a feeling of an elevated transcendence, and they both found themselves with tears running down their faces.

When this lovely man left, she wheeled my friend back to the room and both were laughing with such lightheartedness that the nurses asked, "What happened out there?" When the medical staff hooked him back up, they stood in amazement, for his heart was beating normally and all traces of the A-fib rhythm was gone. They never found out who this gentleman was, nor did they ever see him again. They called him their angel. It sounds to me that he fit the bill.

I've just touched on a smattering of information available about angels. But I've said all of that to say we are so blessed to have angels truly all around us but moving mostly unseen as God directs. I am fascinated that God made these unique and wonderful creatures not only for Himself but also for us. Numerous times, my family, children, husband, or I escaped certain catastrophe by no explainable means other than unseen angels. I bless God for allowing this protection and comfort.

Because of my unshakable belief, if and when I meet you, my reader, more than likely when we part, I will say to you, "Angels around you, dear friend, and God bless you!"

Father God, our great physician, thank You for sending angels, angels we actually recognize and some we wonder about. We thank You for Your healing love and the many rescues You have granted us. We appreciate with our whole being these unforgettable events that You have allowed. Help us to be aware and gracious when entertaining strangers so that we may not miss the opportunity of showing hospitality to angels. In Jesus's name, amen.

Help! The Sky Is Falling!

"Rejoice in the Lord always. I will say it again: Rejoice! Let your gentleness be evident to all. The Lord is near. Do not be anxious about anything, but in every situation, by prayer and petition, with thanksgiving, present your requests to God. And the peace of God, which transcends all understanding, will guard your hearts and your minds in Christ Jesus. Finally, brothers and sisters, whatever is true, whatever is noble, whatever is right, whatever is pure, whatever is lovely, whatever is admirable—if anything is excellent or praiseworthy—think about such things."
—Philippians 4:4–8 (NIV)

Whenever I feel the sky is falling, I always know someone who is far worse off than me, do what I can to help even if it's just prayer, and am thankful for my own familiar troubles and many blessings. Believe me, it wasn't and isn't that easy. It's just a small part of what helps get me over it. This is the way of life—the seesaw that keeps us breathless about what could come next. Sometimes, it's a belly laugh of unexpected hilarity, and other times, it brings sobbing, grief, and concern. No matter what, our God shores us up. When I think I cannot handle one more thing, I hang onto 1 Corinthians 10:13 (NIV), which promises us He will not let us be overcome with more than we can bear without providing strength to endure.

No temptation has overtaken you except what is common to mankind. And God is faithful; he will not let you be tempted beyond what you can bear. But when you are tempted, he will also provide a way out so that you can endure it.

Almost invariably, finding something to do for someone in need will bring me out of it even if it's just a phone call to a shut-in. I find that when I do that, in trying to cheer them, I am often the one who is bolstered. It's not a bad idea to be kind to yourself until you regain your balance, surround yourself with familiar comforts, and perhaps seek out your favorite person and accept a little TLC. Let the dust settle.

My favorite scripture while raising three teenagers with my husband working in Florida, Philippians 4:13 (NIV), assured me then and assures me now that I can do all things through Christ, who strengthens me. Philippians 4:4 (NIV) became my mantra: *"Rejoice in the Lord always and again I say rejoice!"*

In the Name of the Father, the Son, and the Holy Spirit

Therefore go and make disciples of all nations, baptizing them in the name of the Father and of the Son and of the Holy Spirit, and teaching them to obey everything I have commanded you. And surely I am with you always, to the very end of the age.

—Matthew 28:19–20 (NIV)

I love the story in the New Testament in Acts about a wealthy Ethiopian eunuch who in fact was a VIP as treasurer to Candace, the queen of Ethiopia. He was traveling a desert road from Jerusalem to Gaza and sincerely seeking the truth, studying Isaiah the prophet, and puzzling over the part that read, "the lamb that was slaughtered." God was watching and knew the eunuch's heart; He was touched enough that He dispatched an angel to Philip to direct him immediately to the eunuch, and lo, Philip appeared to him and asked if he understood what he was reading. After Philip explained the passage and taught him about Jesus and what it meant to believe, to repent of his sins, and to be baptized, the eunuch said, *"Look, here is water. What can stand in the way of my being baptized?" (Acts 8:36 NIV).*

I find it interesting that water appeared along that dry, dusty desert landscape close to the road and enough for them to walk into and to immerse the eunuch in baptism—fabulous! Once the eunuch knew the truth, he didn't let any grass grow before he wanted to obey. Here's what it says in Acts 8:38–39 (NIV) about the baptism.

> *And he gave orders to stop the chariot. Then both Philip and the eunuch went down into the water and Philip baptized him. When they came up out of the water, the Spirit of the Lord suddenly took Philip away, and the eunuch did not see him again, but went on his way rejoicing.*

Luke 15:10 (NIV) tells us, *"In the same way, I tell you, there is rejoicing in the presence of the angels of God over one sinner who repents."* What a sight that must be! What is standing in the way of your being baptized if you haven't been? I know that's a bold question, but I am old, and I have less time than ever to share the Lord and the path to salvation if you are not on it. And like Father God Himself as represented in the Bible verse below, I want to go to heaven and take everyone with me!

> *The Lord is not slow in keeping his promise, as some understand slowness. Instead he is patient with you, not wanting anyone to perish, but everyone to come to repentance. (2 Peter 3:9 NIV)*

One very good man who had never been baptized explained that he wanted to get it together himself and not use God as a crutch. Oh my! Would you refuse to go to the doctor and refuse crutches if you broke your leg? We are talking about healing a broken spirit and salvation for eternity here—we are talking about taking away every sin and walking with Him toward infinity and living in Paradise forever. Think about it—a supernatural Father and the Holy Spirit to guide us the rest of our lives.

Another person said to me that Jesus was baptized once and that was enough for us all. He must have been mixed up about baptism and the Crucifixion. Christ died once for us and took on all our sins to make a way for us to spend eternity with Him. His baptism by John was not for remission of sins as we do for us because He was without sin; He was baptized out of obedience and to fulfill all righteousness (fulfilling prophecies that the Messiah was coming) as He explained to John in Matthew 3:13–17 (NIV).

> Then Jesus came from Galilee to the Jordan to be baptized by John. But John tried to deter him, saying, "I need to be baptized by you, and do you come to me?"
>
> Jesus replied, "Let it be so now; it is proper for us to do this to fulfill all righteousness." Then John consented.
>
> As soon as Jesus was baptized, he went up out of the water. At that moment heaven was opened, and he saw the Spirit of God descending like a dove and alighting on him. And a voice from heaven said, "This is my Son, whom I love; with him I am well pleased."

John said,

> "I myself did not know him, but for this purpose I came baptizing with water, that he might be revealed to Israel." And John bore witness: "I saw the Spirit descend from heaven like a dove, and it remained on him. I myself did not know him, but he who sent me to baptize with water said to me, 'He on whom you see the Spirit descend and remain, this is he who baptizes with the Holy Spirit.' And I have seen and have borne witness that this is the Son of God." (John 1:31–34 NIV)

People have all sorts of excuses about baptism, but there is verse after verse specifically instructing and commanding baptism to ensure salvation. Just before the ascension in Matthew 28, Jesus commanded it as recorded at the beginning of this essay. Here are just a few more of many verses.

Peter replied, "Repent and be baptized, every one of you, in the name of Jesus Christ for the forgiveness of your sins. And you will receive the gift of the Holy Spirit." (Acts 2:38 NIV)

And this water symbolizes baptism that now saves you also- not the removal of dirt from the body but the pledge of a clear conscience toward God. It saves you by the resurrection of Jesus Christ. (1 Peter 3:21 NIV)

So he ordered that they be baptized in the name of Jesus Christ. Then they asked Peter to stay with them for a few days. (Acts 10:48 NIV)

And now what are you waiting for? Get up, be baptized and wash your sins away, calling on his name. (Acts 22:16 NIV)

For all of you who were baptized into Christ have clothed yourselves with Christ. (Galatians 3:27 NIV)

Whoever believes and is baptized will be saved, but whoever does not believe will be condemned. (Mark 16:16 NIV)

There is one body and one Spirit, just as your were called to one hope when you were called; one Lord, one faith, one baptism; one God and Father of all, who is over all and through all and in all. (Ephesians 4:4–6 NIV)

They replied, "Believe in the Lord Jesus, and you will be saved—you and your household." Then they spoke the word of the Lord to him and to all the others in his house. At that hour of the night, the jailer took them and washed their wounds; then immediately he and all his household were baptized. (Acts 16:31–33 NIV)

Peter replied, "Repent and be baptized, every one of you, in the name of Jesus Christ for the forgiveness of your sins.

And you will receive the gift of the Holy Spirit. The promise is for you and your children and for all who are far off—for all whom the Lord our God will call." With many other words he warned them; and he pleaded with them, "Save yourselves from this corrupt generation." Those who accepted his message were baptized, and about three thousand were added to their number that day. (Acts 2:38–41 NIV)

I've used this example before, but it's worth repeating. If Acts 2:38 read that Peter replied, "Repent and be baptized every one of you in the name of Jesus Christ for the forgiveness of your sins and you will receive the gift of $500,000," I am doubtful many people would delay or refuse baptism.

Think! We are being offered the chance to repent and be baptized for the gift of salvation and to live forever in heaven. We are being offered the gift of the Holy Spirit, and He will bestow power, comfort, healing, and strength—all ours to use immediately here on earth. Yet some are still reluctant.

The issue of baptism is a common question about the thief on the cross who was saved but had not been baptized. He was crucified on a cross next to Jesus, and there is recorded his short talk with Jesus acknowledging his belief and asking Him to remember him. Jesus recognized the thief's belief and his repentant heart, so He told him he would be with Him in Paradise that day. No, he wasn't baptized by water, but he had the ultimate baptism of Jesus's promise that day.

And why not? Jesus, the son of our God, is our Judge. He had the supernatural ability to see this man's heart, and voila! He saved him. That is His prerogative. God knows and loves those who have not been baptized and who we know are good people, in fact wonderful people, and He loves them more than we do. We can take comfort in knowing God is just. But meanwhile, for ourselves, if we know what Jesus instructed and are aware of time after time in the Bible how we are commanded to do that—the simple acts of obedience, confession, and baptism—but continue to refuse to obey, what do you think? I think we should all obey and be baptized without delay as soon as we learn that's what Jesus asked us to do.

I am no Bible scholar, and I am still learning from my own study of the scriptures. Out of love, I wanted to share my thoughts on baptism with any who might benefit. I want to go to heaven and take everyone I know with me!

Father God, again I approach Your throne of grace. Please let my words be acceptable to You and to those who might benefit. Let Your mercy help them find You and Your immeasurable love. In Jesus's name, always Your will be done, amen.

Winter

Here it is—a tired time of cold and dark and old, dead leaves and bare, twisted branches. All outdoors is brown and grey and naked. Winter is the only time the ugly is transformed into the pristine, white loveliness of a thick blanket of snow. The landscape is turned into an awe-inspiring work of art embellished with glittering snow and dripping icicles. Winter blows the breath of clean, pure air that pinks the cheeks and sparkles the eyes. Suddenly, Christmas is here with all its redemptive powers of blazing fires and the scents of pine and turkey baking and cranberry sauce simmering on the stove. Oh the lights of Christmas, those magical lights that would simply fade in summertime.

So I've arrived right smack dab in the middle of the winter of my life before I "slip gently into that good night." I told myself I wouldn't be old till I was eighty. Well, I'm old and past old by a couple of years. At times, it feels like a time warp, for didn't we celebrate our twenty-fifth anniversary just a couple of years ago? How can I remember so clearly my new husband and me picking out a new stove and refrigerator the first week of our marriage over sixty years ago?

Other times, it feels just right, and I feel in the right time and in the right (even if decrepit) body and still in my right mind (though some might debate that). Though the weight of my years is heavy, I feel that those years were rightly spent.

So, Father God, if there is any wisdom, encouragement, or joy that I have gleaned, help me pass it on to my readers. You know I write in love, and I ask You to pour Your hope and joy into my readers as they read until they are filled to overflowing. In His holy name, Your will be done always, amen.

In the Dark Night of the Soul

No trial has overtaken you that is not faced by others. And God is faithful: He will not let you be tried beyond what you are able to bear, but with the trial will also provide a way out so that you may be able to endure it.

—1 Corinthians 10:13 (NET)

Today, our family received grievous news, and I was suddenly slammed with the indelible memory of past hours of agony. It was the dark night of my soul, and I believed I might never breathe again. I remember the thirst that no drink could quench, the emptiness that cried out to be filled. The pain in my heart and in the depth of my being was so intense that I stretched myself out over my kitchen table as far as my arms could reach in supplication, but the hollow ache remained. My tears filled buckets, and the chaos in my mind felt intrusive and noisy. I was on unsteady ground, and the earth shook with tremors no one else felt. Worst of all, I couldn't pray.

But You, dear Holy Spirit, took over for me. I took my Bible and opened it, lay on my bed flat on my back, and laid the scriptures on my chest close to my heart. I uttered as I had many times before and many times since, **"Help me, Jesus."**

The Spirit helps us in our weakness. We do not know what we ought to pray for, but the Spirit himself intercedes for us through wordless groans. (Romans 8:26 NIV)

Though I felt very alone, I knew that in that dark time I was not alone—Father God was with me. Looking back, I know the Holy Spirit had kept me grounded when I thought I might defy gravity and just fly off the earth.

If you are walking that dark path of pain today, you know it isn't always death that brings despair. Divorce often feels like a death; a child in trouble deals one of the worst blows whether it be rebelliousness, injury, illness—Shakespeare said, "Sharper than a serpent's tooth is a thankless child"—a devastating medical report, or a financial loss. I know someone who lost all his savings, and recovering emotionally as well as financially had been a major process for that person.

Whatever the blow to you or your loved ones, while the earth shakes, Father God is immovable, so hang on and listen for His plan. Here are some of the scriptures that helped me and may help you.

> *The righteous cry out, and the LORD hears, And delivers them out of all their troubles. (Psalm 34:17 NIV)*

> *You, dear children, are from God and have overcome them, because the one who is in you is greater than the one who is in the world. (1 John 4:4 NIV)*

> *You are my hiding place; You shall preserve me from trouble; You shall surround me with songs of deliverance. Selah. (Psalm 32:7 NIV)*

> *Many are the afflictions of the righteous, But the Lord delivers him out of them all. (Psalm 34:19 NIV)*

> *The steps of a good man are ordered by the Lord, And He delights in his way. Though he fall, he shall not be utterly cast down; For the Lord upholds him with His hand. (Psalm 37:23–24 NIV)*

He also brought me up out of a horrible pit, Out of the miry clay, And set my feet upon a rock, And established my steps. (Psalm 40:2 NIV)

As my Gramma Sullivan used to say, "Jes' keep on keeping on." Put one foot in front of the other. Be extremely kind to yourself, drink plenty of water, and eat proteins (smoothies and yogurt). Find your softest pillow and comforter and try hard to rest—sleep if you can. Gather only the help you trust, and make very few big decisions except what you have to.

Back in the seventies, Norman Cousins was diagnosed with a terminal and extremely painful illness. He determined to change his miserable life, and he moved to a hotel next to the hospital and rented movies—comedies. He spent two hours a day in what he called belly-ripping laughter, and he was healed.

Years later, he wrote his story, *The Anatomy of an Illness*. There was even a movie made of it. I believe his method is valid today. Rent funny movies and laugh as much as you can, go for long walks along beautiful pathways, and eat an ice cream cone on one of those strolls. Buy yourself some beautiful flowers once a week. Whatever brings positivity and even a short respite from the ongoing darkness will eventually help point you toward wholeness again.

Remember always that things change in a blink of an eye. Remember the trials of the past God has seen you through. Remember the strength that He always gives you.

Father God, tonight, I pray for the hurting, for the confused, for the grieving, and for those who are dealing with issues that cause pain, and please remove all fear. Father, You know Your children and their needs. Be what they need right now and supply it, show them their path, and please comfort their families. Father, whatever they are lacking, fill it now to overflowing in Your great goodness. Father, Your Son knows the agonies we endure, and He too grieves for our pain. In Your mercy, please shorten this time of pain and bring healing. In the name of Jesus, Your will always be done, amen.

Old Songs, New Songs

He put a new song in my mouth, a hymn of praise to our God.
—*Psalm 40:3 (NIV)*

One night not long ago, I clicked on fifties music for some reason and played so many nostalgic tunes—Rosemary Clooney singing "Blue Moon," "Tenderly," "Come Onna My House," Bobby Darin singing "Mack the Knife," and many more. I decided sleep wasn't that important right that minute and just gave in to the total pleasure of listening to marvelous, worshipful music. I watched about an hour of *The Best of Guy Penrod*, which was not only inspirational music but also about his family and home life. Lots of songs that were new to me too!

After many more Gaither songs, songs and hymns my daddy led in singing in the little church where I'd grown up, and songs my sisters and I harmonized on, I finally turned in at 3:00 a.m. My back hurt, and I was exhausted, but my spirit was soaring! I felt as if I were twenty again but with sixty years of love behind it. Worth it? Yes. I am holding onto this filling up of my soul and spirit and drinking in all the beauty and love God is pouring on me right now to guard against the next storm that will surely come.

But for now, Father, I am singing Your new song along with the old. Praise You forever, Father!

Christmas

Today in the town of David a Savior has been born to you;
he is the Messiah, the Lord. This will be a sign to you: You
will find a baby wrapped in cloths and lying in a manger.
Suddenly a great company of the heavenly host appeared
with the angel, praising God and saying, "Glory to God in
the highest heaven, and on earth peace to those on whom his
favor rests."

—Luke 2:11–14 (NIV)

Once again, in my mind I hear the old, gentle, tinkling melody of "Silver Bells." I hear the church bell in the little Baptist church in Fullerton on Sunday mornings tolling, "Come to church, come to church." I picture bell ringers in their robes, their soft, loose, black ties, and those white gloves chiming in perfect harmony, "I Heard the Bells on Christmas Day."

Christmas carols remind us of angels singing in heaven to herald His arrival. We give gifts reminiscent of the wise men honoring the Messiah with their priceless frankincense and myrrh. Sparkling lights recall the star of Bethlehem and the Light of the World. I love this season. I cherish concerts and caroling, catching whiffs of pine and candles burning, hot cider simmering on the stove, peppermint candy canes, and children's faces looking in wonder at Christmas lights.

I remember past Christmases watching a TV video of a medley of bells from all over the world ringing in a beautiful symphony of celebration and praise. As the reverberation of bells faded, there fell a stunning silence of peace. And that was forever my Christmas message this lovely season of the year—peace, that calm quiet during which we all heard only the language of love.

In remembering Christ's birth, I am thinking of Mary, His mother. Somehow, the older I become, the clearer visual I have of that blessed young woman most likely ostracized for being pregnant; even Joseph doubted her at first. I think of the desert heat and cold with no air conditioning or heaters, of the daily hard work of survival, and preparing meals with no kitchen or Schwan's trucks to deliver frozen dinners. No warm showers, no Kleenex, and no washers or dryers.

How did Mary endure riding on a donkey those many miles with the baby's delivery imminent, surely in pain from contractions and the fatigue of pregnancy with no waiting clean, warm bed? How in the world did they manage diapers? I am in awe of how she kept her peace and how the grace of God sent the angel to Joseph so he too could believe and confidently protect her. What must they have thought to have this world-shaking event placed upon them, these simple yet chosen people? What did they imagine when the shepherds sought them out to worship and adore the babe and the wise men came from afar bringing rich gifts?

How did they feel when they received urgent heavenly instructions to flee immediately to save their Son, the sovereign Son of God Himself? King Herod and his henchmen killed hundreds of babies to try to eliminate the miraculous Immaculate Conception, Jesus, the Son God gave Mary to raise.

Joseph and Mary accepted God's will and listened and obeyed in total faith; they trusted God with every step. But they were humans, and their parents' hearts surely trembled. They were just like us, but they were committed to Him. They were perfect examples of people living their faith and rising far above my stumbling efforts.

I am staggered as I remember Christ and why He left the glories of heaven in obedience to be born in poverty to an immaculate virgin and live in a human body. He experienced just how we lived and how we felt, but He submitted to the agonizing cross so we might live eternally.

He rose to life again miraculously, forever proving His sonship and fulfilling the magnificent promise of heaven. Staying in the Word and meditating on Christ's life and death make the very air I breathe more precious, knowing His immense sacrifice for all of us.

So what do I say to the naysayers for various reasons who deny Christmas at all for themselves and their families? My answer is Philippians 1:18 (NIV): "But what does it matter? The important thing is that in every way, whether from false motives or true, Christ is preached. And because of this I rejoice. Yes, and I will continue to rejoice."

And that's all I have to say about that. I snuggle by my fireplace, wrap myself in the afghan a friend made me, feel the peace of the season steal over me, and keep Christmas simple in my own way in my heart and home, not forgetting the reason for the season—praising Him for His grace and glory.

Heavenly Father, thank You for allowing most of the world to stop in praise and thanksgiving that our Savior was born. Help us set aside gifts and feasting and parties to immerse ourselves in praise time and worship time ever grateful for His birth. Help us to let the beauty of the season envelop us and just enjoy the reason we are celebrating. Thank You for sending Your Son to earth to live as a human being and thus gain complete understanding of us. Thank You for granting us the freedom to choose to live with You forever. In His holy name, Your will be done forever, amen.

Unto One of the Least of These

Then the King will say to those on his right, "Come, you who are blessed by my Father; take your inheritance, the kingdom prepared for you since the creation of the world. For I was hungry and you gave me something to eat, I was thirsty and you gave me something to drink, I was a stranger and you invited me in, I needed clothes and you clothed me, I was sick and you looked after me, I was in prison and you came to visit me."

Then the righteous will answer him, "Lord, when did we see you hungry and feed you, or thirsty and give you something to drink? When did we see you a stranger and invite you in, or needing clothes and clothe you? When did we see you sick or in prison and go to visit you?" The King will reply, "Truly I tell you, whatever you did for one of the least of these brothers and sisters of mine, you did for me."
—Matthew 25:34–40 (NIV)

Remembering my gramma, my mother's mother, is a warm fuzzy for me. She was exactly that—warm and comforting—and I never heard a negative word about her. Mama told me that when she was a little girl, they lost their farm in Missouri and moved to Arkansas to work a sharecropper farm close to the railroad. Daily, there were hungry men riding the rails who came to Gramma's back door to ask for food.

Financially, Gramma and her family were at poverty level, but on the farm, there was always food. She fed every single man who asked.

Some of the men worked for their food by doing some sort of chore, but she told her family that she would not burden some of the weariest men for they looked "done in," she said. She would tell the worn-out travelers that she had an able-bodied husband, ten children—eight of her own and two of her brother's children—so she had plenty of help.

In the early 1940s, my family and I lived close to a barranca, a flood-control channel that to our surprise ended in a hobo haven for transients quite close to us. One adventurous time, one of my older sister's young male friends from college took my little sister and me on a hike clear past the end of the barranca. There, we witnessed makeshift shelters in a jungle-like tangle of trees and bushes only a couple of miles from our house. It was exciting for us and a little scary to have such a foreign element so close to our home!

So we were conveniently close for a fast-food "stop" for several of the men, and Mama never turned them away. Transients regularly tapped on the back door of our nice little home with Daddy's immaculate yard and pretty flowers. They were always quiet, humble, and very hungry. I remember that Mama never turned one away; she always fixed a huge, filling meal for them. She used her large fried chicken platter to serve them, and she usually filled it with two big ham or fried baloney or tuna salad sandwiches, a huge pile of quickly fried-up potatoes, and a quart of milk. At times, there was a big slice of homemade pie, or a huge square of chocolate cake, or a handful of cookies. Almost always, she'd give them an apple or banana to shove in their pockets "for later."

Mama, who had been raised on a farm, was a believer in big breakfasts, and our visitors became wise to her wonderful early morning meals. Whoever showed up was in for a treat, and she filled that big platter with bacon or sausage and fried eggs, her light-as-a-feather biscuits, homemade jam or Karo syrup and butter, and cup after cup of boiled coffee usually topped off with cinnamon toast or pie. They would sit on the back steps or sometimes at the picnic table on the patio and feast.

Daddy said our home had been "marked" by the transients because

Mama was so generous. In my memory, we had a parade of men from time to time for a good long while, and we girls were severely warned to leave them alone and not talk with them. Oh what a hardship it was for me to keep my mouth shut! On occasion, Daddy had them chop a load of firewood or rake the leaves, but mostly, they just wished them well and sent them on their way, filled and grateful.

I grew up in the church, and I learned there were always the needy or sick. Mama would take a couple of quart jars of her good soup and a big, yellow, crusty cake of cornbread from her black iron skillet and away we would go, we two little girls in the back of our '36 two-door Chevy sedan with that prickly horsehair upholstery. Sometimes, she would let us carry the goodies to the door, but usually not, for she didn't want us to "catch anything."

I remember as a little girl of maybe nine sewing buttons on used clothing and folding a never-ending pile of wearables for the needy. Every few months, there were boxes of clothes in the garage ready for whomever. A much older cousin in Arkansas lost her home in a fire, and though they were not hurt, they needed everything. Mother and the women of the church in Fullerton put together four huge boxes of everything imaginable they could collect for that young family with children.

I rode with Mama to the railroad station where she summoned men from the station to carry those big, heavy boxes in for sending by rail. My cousin was astounded, dumbfounded with gratitude at the willingness of complete strangers to help them in their need.

When I was about eight, a very young couple with an infant came to our church; they were flat broke and unemployed. Our home was tiny—two bedrooms and a small bathroom—but it housed the five of us quite well even if we were scrunched a little. But our garage was rather large with a small bedroom and makeshift bathroom—a toilet and very rough shower. The people who built our house had lived there temporarily while they built the main house.

Mama and Daddy let this young couple stay in that garage apartment for about two weeks; they fed them and worked hard to bring them back to health. They were probably not over twenty; they were silent, frightened, thin, pale, and frail. Mama asked our doctor to treat them for free, and he did, and Daddy bought the baby's medicine plus baby formula because the young mother's breast milk had dried up.

My little sister and I were threatened within an inch of our lives to stay away lest we caught whatever they had, but otherwise, my parents were overly generous with them. There really was no extra money, and indeed, my older sister, just a teenager herself, worked after school to help make ends meet. Mama did their wash, cooked for them, and gave them a quick course in Newborn 101. She gathered clothes and necessities for them from the ever-giving women at church.

After two weeks, they were looking sturdier and a little less frightened. Daddy handed them ten of his hard-earned dollars and bid them adieu. The elders from church picked them up, and lo! They had found him a job in a nearby town.

Mama and Daddy never learned another thing about them; they never really had a conversation with them except when instructing them on life in general. Daddy said the young man mumbled, "Thank you" as they left, and their story remained a mystery.

Looking back from my vantage point of old age, those poor kids were obviously at their rock bottom, paralyzed, and not knowing what to say or do. They were too immature and unschooled to even interact with their benefactors. I think God sent them to Mama and Daddy knowing they would be well looked after.

Though we were young, JoAn and I were incensed at the whole thing for we thought they had taken terrible advantage of us. But Mama told us that she had never cast her bread upon the water that it didn't come back to her tenfold, and she knew God knew, and that was all that mattered. That was the very first time I ever heard that expression, but I often heard her repeat it through the years after that.

She also reminded us of the ancient and intriguing scripture I have never forgotten: *"Do not forget to show hospitality to strangers, for by so doing some people have shown hospitality to angels without knowing it" (Hebrews 13:2 NIV).* With such a family background, I found it as natural as breathing to help others, and I was blessed that my husband was generous and shared my aspirations in that regard. I almost always found it fun and rewarding, and usually, both of us were working, so it wasn't a huge financial hardship for us.

Several years ago, my daughter and I became aware of a young family of three who were expecting twins any day. They didn't have much of anything, especially clothes, diapers, or blankets for the little ones who would be arriving shortly. We stopped and prayed about it, and we were in that car and at Ross for Less in a blink of an eye; what a blessed, fun time we had! We bought four or five complete layettes for each baby, cuddly blankets, and lots of diapers. I burned up a credit card tickled that I had it to use. What a gratifying moment my daughter had when she presented our gift to the grateful parents.

My husband and I shared mostly by taking in whoever needed sheltering in our home for however long—maybe a few weeks, maybe a few months, and sometimes even years. My mama said to me more than once that we ran McDaniel's Bed and Breakfast.

Today in every town are homeless people who need blankets, jackets or coats, gloves, and hats. There are free or almost free kitchens that feed the homeless, and my sister is one who cooked meals once a week for such a kitchen. Even though she was working full time and was a mother of four, she volunteered at the convalescent center shampooing and setting hair for patients for a long time. She is the ultimate in generosity.

My aunt and uncle moved to another state after they retired, and they cooked for Meals on Wheels for ten years. My older sister and her husband financed a needy family for many years until the children were grown and able to work. Our church maintains a clothing closet—a huge room—managed by a precious woman who has poured out her time and energy on organizing, cleaning, and distributing excellent used clothing in a once-a-month neighborhood giveaway in our church's parking lot. People pitch in to help, but she's the guiding light, and the closet is cleaned out in the giveaway every month. There will always be the needy, and there will always be a place to help out.

I was so pleased that my church had an outreach to the correctional facility in our community. A dear couple, our minister, our church secretary, and a select few from the congregation held Bible lessons and counseling at the prison for many years. My husband and I became close friends with them, and we had our own private Bible lessons with just the four of us in our home for about a year and a half.

During that time, it became evident that they had such a passion for teaching prisoners and bringing not only hope and a touch of normality to their lives but also salvation to many. They were a dear, hard-working couple whose loss was so painful when they eventually moved. Fortunately, we still keep in touch. Our Bible says, *"I needed clothes and you clothed me, I was sick and you looked after me, I was in prison and you came to visit me" Matthew 25:36 (NIV).*

I felt a need to write about hospitality and caring for the less fortunate because it was on my heart to encourage those of you who might not participate to find even a small amount of time, clothing, or money every month or so and get involved. When all of us give just a little, collectively, that pays enormous dividends to the recipients and lets those who have done the giving experience a huge feeling of reward. And while God does not keep track of our repented misdeeds, He records every good deed we do! He tells us plainly that when we do it for those in need, we do it for Him.

Father, help us today to see the need, and nudge us to fill those empty places as we are able. Help us to use our own special talents in the areas You direct us. Thank You for sending help when we ourselves needed it, and now guide us to do what You would have us do for others. In His name, Your will be done, amen.

A Prayer of Praise and Thanksgiving

Do not be anxious about anything, but in every situation, by prayer and petition, with thanksgiving, present your requests to God.

—Philippians 4:6 (NIV)

Awesome Father, gracious God, Creator of my world and all of creation, I praise You for this world, this universe where You made eternity, unknown worlds beyond ours, in the celestial magnificence of the heavens.

Praise You also for making me and my loved ones and for the huge sacrifice of Your Son so we can be together forever. Thank You for the Holy Spirit and for His indwelling. Thank You for the industrious ant, for the giant whale, for puppies and kittens, the praying mantis, and for the delight they bring when we watch them.

Father, I confess, as You already know, that I am undisciplined, and at times, in the midst of overwhelming blessings, I cry with self-pity. Forgive me, please, for these and a thousand other shortcomings. As much as I love You and have served You, I could have done better.

Help me now in my weakness and in the winter of my life to give You only my best. Please help me with an ever-stronger faith, and help my aging, broken body. Let my smile, peace, joy, and faith be evident and always reflect Your precious love. My help, hope, and expectation of my home in heaven all lie in You. I cannot tell You enough of my gratitude, my great and wonderful counselor. Abba Father, Jehovah, El-Shaddai, Elohim, the great I Am.

In a New Land

The LORD your God is in your midst, a mighty one who will
save; he will rejoice over you with gladness; he will quiet you
by his love; he will exult over you with loud singing.
                                        —Zephaniah 3:17 (NIV)

I am in a strange land, new to me, a land I call the Back of Beyond. In my eighty-first year, I took my first airplane trip and flew from my California home to Montana to live out the rest of my days with my oldest daughter and son-in-law.

I came from a relatively quiet central-coast town, but it was full of hustle and bustle compared to the quiet isolation of my new central Montana home. I found that God was there way ahead of me and welcomed me with sunsets and sunrises that blew me away!

For instance, this morning, I hear a *ping, ping, ping* that is musical and rhythmic from the dripping raindrops leftover from this morning's passing showers; they are like lovely notes of a song to the sunrise. In the east, there is the pink-orange tint that stretches long miles across the horizon under a lavender sky. A lone bird flies swiftly upward flapping wings furiously and flinging a lonely warbling birdsong into the quiet and ever-brightening air. That bird, the growing brilliant colors in the east, and I know that the sun is near. It's as if I can hear a dozen violins playing a long, drawn-out, suspenseful note—an anticipatory prelude that is sustained and dramatic and leads up to the crashing musical trumpet tones that finally announce in blindingly yellow-white transcendence, "Ta dah! Day has arrived, ladies and gentlemen. Make it a good one."

There are things in this world and in the world to come too wonderful, too omnipotent for our comprehension. Even with Him bestowing me with the "mind of Christ", even after all the years I've witnessed amazing things, never do I grow complaisant. I am ever and continually gobsmacked at our God, at Jesus, at the Holy Spirit. I think the spirit of being able to live in wonder is so renewing day by day, so much the tabasco in spicing up the sometimes blandness in the regularity of life. I love the thrill of the day unfolding and its unpredictability and yet, at the same time, the comforting predictability of sunrises and sunsets with the continual blatant uniqueness of each one. The sameness and the difference is mind-blowing when contemplating the mind of the Creator. Even if it is the natural progression of what God set in motion, it is still God-breathed and miraculous to me.

It is not a defined New Testament miracle, but looking out my window and seeing a mama doe with her newborn twin fawns interacting sparks a gratitude in me that makes me as thankful as If I am indeed witnessing and miracle. And so, to me a miracle; to you providential. Makes no never-mind as my Gramma used to say. We are here by the grace of that omniscient Creator and exist from the breath He blew into us. God is, He was, and He will be forevermore. He is the Great I AM and in every cell, every heart beat, every leaf that unfurls and every cloud that rains or doesn't rain. The "very rocks cry out" proclaiming Him. For that, I am grateful and enjoy everyday "miracles" that enhance the very air I breathe.

Father God, tomorrow, Your sunrise will be different but equally as lovely, and You do this day upon endless day. Thank You for the ever-the-same, ever-changing scenes You produce in glorious drama. Unbelievably, I think, this is all free for me to absorb in wonder—me, an insignificant ant who looks up in awe

at an overwhelmingly blessed world, and I realize, amazingly, that You love even me.

Father, as I adjust to my new Land of Canaan, in Your mercy, grant me the ability and the willingness to conform to new schedules, a different climate, and finding my niche in Montana. Help me to love it and to fulfill whatever mission You have for me here.

I am old and not as productive, but I know You've kept me alive for a purpose, so help me do whatever it is You planned for me. Thank You for the conscientious care I am so lovingly given. Your will be done, in Jesus's name, amen.

Spending Our Time

Teach us to number our days, that we may gain a heart of wisdom.

—Psalm 90:12 (NIV)

Can we measure our days and count the "wins" we have each day? These days, I am much aware of numbering my days; at this time in my life, I know there's a lot less left now than before. As a young wife and mother and through middle age (but not so much now in my "dotage"), I often experienced flat-out, backbreaking schedules, some no fault of mine, but much of it was exactly because of me.

What I am most pleased with are the times I felt God's calling and I said yes to Him. What I am less proud of are the times I ignored my husband's plea for a little less busywork that infringed on family time and not having invoked my powerful no that God gives us freedom to use at the proper times. Only now do I understand that my mistaken notion of making those many casseroles, teaching yet again another class, and saying, "Yes, I'll decorate for the upcoming youth forum" did not necessarily secure my place in heaven.

God blessed me with a husband, three children, a home, and all that those elements entailed. Keeping that home, rocking my babies, and making our nest a soft spot to fall—while very important to me—didn't seem enough then. I didn't realize how fast the children would be grown and *pffffft!*—gone. I added a full-time job to help my husband. I added Sunday school, decorating for church functions, sewing all my kids' clothes, being a room mother, being a Little League mother, piano lessons, drum lessons, ballet, softball, baseball—and all the shuttling back and forth those tasks required of me.

I do not object to wives and mothers working outside the home; that's often a necessity, and it must be an individual family's choice. And I know my busywork was good. But because of what we as a family missed—long and quiet times together—and because my health suffered, in hindsight, I now advocate setting priorities—God first, and then you and your spouse, family, church, and community. Your scheduling might call for major adjustments—quietly watching the sun set, long walks and picnics, singing to the kids, playing dress-up, committing God's Word to memory, watching clouds flat on your back on a summer day, building a lemonade stand, reading Robert Louis Stevenson to the children, and such. These can get shoved aside when there is an outside agenda. When you try to fit them into an overly scheduled life, there goes the peace, which is the whole point in the first place. Extracurriculars might be better left for when the kids leave home.

For now, take the measure of your days, fill them with God's timely work, and pencil in lots of spare recesses—times for just sittin' and rockin' and contemplating the sunset. God loves for us to be still and know that He is God.

Father God, our Creator, we know You rested on the seventh day. Help us be wise enough to know when to rest as well. Help us refocus on what You would set as our priorities. Help us keep You first in our lives, and then take care of the precious families You gave us. Help us keep our jobs in perspective—necessary for our living but not our first priority. In Jesus's name, amen.

Friends

Two are better than one, because they have a good return
for their work; If one falls down, his friend can help him up.
But pity the man who falls and has no one to help him up!
—Ecclesiastes 4:9–10 (NIV)

Friendship. The word itself is comforting to me because it speaks of my childhood pals and I playing jacks on our knees, giggling teen girls sharing secrets, and stalwart adult friends whose support, prayers, and hugs shored me up time and again.

God has blessed me greatly with people in my life to whom I know I can turn, even to call at midnight if I needed. Proverbs 17:17 tells me, "A friend loveth at all times," and I've had that love poured out on me during tragedy but also during good times when we happily hollered with laughter! There are friends for a season who come and go, but the friends who grace my life and mean everything to me have been steadfast and sure for more than fifty years! We might not talk or see each other for a time, but when we do, it's as if no time has passed. We take up where we'd left off, open up to each other, and love each other even more. Here's a quote from Dinah Maria (Mulock) Craik (1820–1887).

> *Oh, the inexpressible comfort of feeling safe with a person:*
> *having neither to weigh thoughts nor measure words, but to*
> *pour them out. Just as they are—chaff and grain together,*
> *knowing that a faithful hand will take and sift them, keep*

what is worth keeping, and then with the breath of kindness,
blow the rest away.

I love you, my friend, because you know me so well that you know my foibles and my fears, my strengths and my weaknesses, but you love me in spite of that. When I fall, your strong arms of belief in me bring me back. How many times have I made it because of your faith and your prayers! You make me better than I would be without you. You know who you are.

Father God, You thought up friendship, and bless You for it! These like-minded loved ones give me renewed hope and steady me through the yin and yang of life. Help me, Father, to be the friend You want me to be, and help me bless them as they have blessed me. In Jesus's name, amen.

Grief, the Shapeshifter

O.K., I tend to call this grief thing a shapeshifter.

After seven years, grief is a quiet aching wound that lives forever in my soul, spirit and body, usually manageable now. Quiescent, it is dignified and holy. After several years, we made an agreement, my grief and I, that after I spent my life in a rather dark maelstrom for at least over two years, it was time I make a new path that would hopefully lead me to a different type of fulfillment. Part of the time it works. Grief quietly rests in a remote corner of my spirit in grace and courage where sacred memories lie soft and fresh under a sheer silken veil of intense love and refined regret. Lovely things happen now; terrible things, too, ever try to take me out but I am more malleable, more resilient; the world turns; friends continue to pour out encouragement; and God gently leads me in the path of righteousness while I try very hard to follow.

With new friends come fresh encouragements and new inspirations. Old friends and family provide the comfort of snuggling into the familiar arms of their mantras: "cry as long as it takes"; "I got your back"; "God never moves"'; "you are stronger than you know"; "there is no time limit to grief"; one I love - "I'm here"; "here's a plan – think it might help?"; and the balm that never fails, "I love you, Joey".

And so, the timetable of my life turns some days so slowly, I think I hear the hum of the mysterious place it begins and ends, and I can even hear a ladybug breathe. Some days it's so breathtakingly fast, I'm confused – is this 7 a.m. or p.m.? I see a baby photo and for a split second, it's 1956 and that's my baby with the helplessly heart melting toothless drooling grin. No wait, my baby is a grandmother! We've jettisoned into the 21st century, and wait! - Trump is my President? Franklin Delano Roosevelt and Eisenhower both are rooted in my mind as honored leaders of my country. Whaaaat happened?

Without warning, the shapeshifter awakes and emanates full power from a TV commercial perhaps about the tender daddy with his beloved child, and there is my Bill, full of life and twinkling brown eyes, and I am consumed with grief, howling out my despair. I am turning a page in our old tattered blue phone book, and there is his handwriting. I fold up, and grief is now the shapeshifter monster from the movie "Poltergeist", and I am the pitiful small heap of despair in front of him. All my beloveds now waiting in heaven, rise from time to time in my fully functioning memory in the full color of their personalities and peculiarities. Now it is my Mama with her bright blue eyes and long pink fingernails that take me to my knees. Tomorrow. my shy Daddy or my grandparents; my beloved Hale and his "squeak"; my precious Shelley; beautiful Tiffany; my childhood best friend; uncles and aunts; Arvella; a really close loving neighbor couple; and lately so many of my cohorts, year after year of saying goodbye to precious friends from church. Silly, but I cried the day Debbie Reynolds died recently.

I find that now that I'm 82 and have a doctor's pronouncement that to some would seem dire, my mind spends some, not a lot of time, imagining our reunion in heaven. I still make plans daily for continuing here a little longer at least, and am not afraid to buy green bananas! There is enough here for me to do that I wake excited about what God has in store for me today! But the splendid reunion is always there, waiting, beckoning in love.

If you haven't had the valley of the shadow of grief yet, just know it will come to you, and your experience will be unique unto you. Hold to God's hand and ask him to guide you, for you will walk a new path. This life is one I absolutely never expected nor prepared for – don't think you can prepare except to keep your love and gratitude going for our Lord and Savior. Different ones I know are grieving differently from me. I had a girlfriend who told me she never cried after the first week. It was demoralizing for her and weakened her and she refused to do it and spent her grieving in remembering good things. Then there's me. I don't know how to NOT cry – at the good things, at the not so good things and everything in between, and that may be you or not.

I know God wants us to be happy and productive, and I know he understands every emotion including sadness. And so my prayer always includes, "Your will be done, Father". With this, I expect paths of happiness, but also strength to endure when it's not happy at all. My motivation now daily is to try to reach out to encourage and to exhort you to as Winston Churchill famously said, nevah, nevah, nevah turn loose of God's hand. In walking this path, I am hopeful I can be of some gentle encouragement and uplifting to all of you. Pray without ceasing, and pray with ultimate gratitude even in your grief, even if it is hard, pray thankfully for, if nothing else, mundane things like Kleenex and Vaseline to soothe your ruined eyes and nose. Be gentle with yourself, and gentle with those who are close to you and grieving. And let us not be offended when our efforts are rebuffed by our loved ones, for they are also in a new place and may not act like they did in the past.

And so, realizing that a shapeshifter is a mythological creature, and one not at all in God's plan, I'm asking Him to help me to remove that scary personage.

Please, Father, let a more gentle grief fold up and remove itself back to that more dignified quiet place in my spirit and let it rest under the veil of loving sacred memories. When my Prince appears and holds out one of his perfect roses to me and twinkles his eyes at me, please Father, let me just enjoy and remember the perfume of the past, and keep grief contained into a more manageable sweet nostalgia.

A Slice of Love

You have searched me, Lord, and you know me. You know when I sit and when I rise; you perceive my thoughts from afar. You discern my going out and my lying down; you are familiar with all my ways. Before a word is on my tongue you, Lord, know it completely.

—Psalm 139:1–4 (NIV)

My daughter sliced up a ripe pineapple and served me several slices. It was delectable; its fragrance was wonderful, and its taste was perfect for that warm, summer day. She remarked that it made her think of no matter how wonderful that pineapple was, how much more marvelous would be the fruit trees of heaven and the banquet our Father was preparing for us. I often think the same; He has blessed us with much now and throughout our lives, but how much more it will be then and forever.

She walked over to my chair with a piece of the rind of the pineapple and said, "Look, Mom!" I was amazed to see the pattern of the fruit left encircling the cut rind formed hearts—connected hearts, one right after the other. I thought, *He knew my daughter would buy that particular pineapple, and He knew that on that particular day, it would be difficult for me having lost my prince not long before.* God reminded me once again in that small, loving, yet significant way just like that circle of hearts on the rind, He has encircled my life with hearts who care, and, once again, I know He cares.

Dear Father, there are days You do something so loving, so unexpected, and so uplifting. This is one of those days. Thank You! In Jesus's name, amen.

Fear Not!

Do not be afraid of those who kill the body but cannot kill the soul. Rather, be afraid of the One who can destroy both soul and body in hell. Are not two sparrows sold for a penny? Yet not one of them will fall to the ground outside your Father's care. And even the very hairs of your head are all numbered. So don't be afraid; you are worth more than many sparrows.
—Matthew 10:28–31 (NIV)

It was a late afternoon, and it was warmer than usual. A summer storm blew up and blasted away at my world for maybe fifteen minutes. A little jiggle of alarm hit the bottom of my tummy. The thunder blasted and crashed so loudly that I jumped, and the nearly simultaneous lightning flashed brilliant, enormous, jagged, sideways bolts that hurt my eyes. Other bolts—wide and straight as tree trunks—bore down into the earth too close for comfort. The wind blew the downpour into horizontal sheets that howled, threatened, and furiously threw enormous drops that sounded like pebbles pounding against my windows. When the power went out, my warm, bright, comfortable nest with my friendly movie keeping me company was suddenly in darkness for the next three hours.

Finally, the storm passed and left a constant flickering of light over the mountains and a low rumbling that was beautiful and comforting—from a distance. I'm a California-raised woman who never experienced seasons outside of the mild and lovely central coast until a little over a year ago when God relocated me to Montana.

I'm in my eighties; I'm a modern pioneer experiencing incredibly beautiful and powerfully different seasons of nature that open my mind to heretofore unknown paths God has planned for me. But with God at my side, I fear not.

> *For God has not given us a spirit of fear and timidity, but of power, love, and self-discipline. (2 Timothy 1:7 NLT)*

In the middle of this chaos, I heard a sweet voice say, "Mom! I'm here!" My daughter did not want me to be alone, and how I welcomed her company and the candles she lit. Of course, it reminded me that I was never really alone. When the storm first began to make me feel apprehensive, I prayed for His presence and protection. Immediately, I knew as I always had known that He was with me.

I have read that there are 365 references in the Bible that urge us to "Fear not!" Later, I read that may not be an accurate count, but even if not, just knowing we are being encouraged over a hundred times in His Word to not be afraid means this is serious business. We can count on Him to never forsake us.

My God is bigger. David confronted Goliath who was dressed in armor and endowed with enormous height and weight compared to David, who couldn't wear the king's armor because it was too big for him. *"David said to the Philistine, 'You come against me with sword and spear and javelin, but I come against you in the name of the LORD Almighty, the God of the armies of Israel, whom you have defied'" (1 Samuel 17:35 NIV). David's declaration gives me chill bumps! "I come against you in the name of the Lord almighty, the God is the armies of Israel."* Of course Goliath was defeated!

When I fight my own Goliaths, I remember not to fear anything because I have the helmet of salvation, the belt of truth, the breastplate of righteous, and all of heaven on my side! (See Ephesians 6:11–14, which describes the whole armor of God.) Sometimes when I quake, it's because I've forgotten that God's holy host of angels is surrounding me.

God, help me and all of us to remember that yes, we are in a holy war against Satan and his demons, but we have the strongest power in the universe—You and Your army fighting for us.

So this brief, stormy time reminds me of all the sudden attacks throughout our lives that come and sometimes do take us to the brink, but He never forsakes us! If we can't go around it, He walks us through it, and in the end, the Holy Spirit comforts us. In our darkest hours, He is there!

One of my favorite passages in all of His Word is Psalm 139:7–10 (NIV). I especially love,

> *Where can I go from your Spirit? Where can I flee from your presence? If I go up to the heavens, you are there; If I make my bed in the depths, you are there. If I rise on the wings of the dawn, if I settle on the far side of the sea, even there your hand will guide me.*

Father, thank You for providing ways of escape in everyday life and that even unto death, You will hold me safe and allow angels to escort me. Bless You, Father, for that reassurance. In His name, amen.

Assembling Ourselves

Not giving up meeting together, as some are in the habit of doing, but encouraging one another—and all the more as you see the Day approaching.

—Hebrews 10:25 (NIV)

Swathed in the gauzy mists of memory are days in my childhood, days in my life, and the hours I spent in church. Some of those days are clear and fresh such as the Wednesday night I met my prince on the front steps of that little church; that is still so vividly pristine and precious in my mind, and the way my heart pounded in my throat that night is unforgettable.

There are warm and comforting earlier remembrances. There were rows of old, dark, wooden theater chairs with the fold-down seats—oh yes! How they cut into the back of my little girl's knees, and no, they were not particularly comfortable. There were long, narrow windows in the auditorium that let in God's warming light through the very old and wavy glass. The smell in that probably one-hundred-year old building was old—old wood and old furniture polish. The bathrooms are not a great memory for they were dark and ancient, all facilities wooden with the flush toilets' wooden tanks mounted precariously high on the wall over our heads. A long pull chain hung from it to flush that worked or sometimes not. Unfortunately, all was smelly and unpleasant.

There was the nursery/primary classroom, a pleasant room with lots of light along one wall from those same long, narrow windows with that old, wavy glass. This was my first classroom where, at age thirteen, I taught my first Sunday school lesson to precious preschoolers. I remember spending hours making a book, drawing and coloring page after page to illustrate the story of creation, Adam and Eve in the garden. I remember the pleasure I felt when the little ones attentively followed that little amateur textbook I'd made for them.

After evening services in the summertime, bats flew helter-skelter from under the roof and around the building scaring us girls half to pieces. But overall, the security I found in the regularity of every Sunday morning and evening, every Wednesday night, and always a week of Vacation Bible School gave me a solidity and expectation that all was right with the world.

I did suffer four years of insecurity in my mind as a frightened little girl because of fear of being bombed during World War II. But an experience as a six-year-old in that little Church of Christ on Harvard and Amerige in Fullerton went a long way in helping making me feel safer in that tiny, old building.

There were a few air-raid warnings at night, and one was exceptional in that it happened during a Wednesday-night church service. Mama and Daddy were insistent that if ever there was a time to rely on God, that was it, and they drove us on the darkened streets to every scheduled service. During the war years, there were no streetlights or the usually warm, welcoming lights coming from houses along the streets because we were under blackout orders to make it more difficult for enemy planes to bomb us at night. Every home and building had to have heavy black drapes pulled over every window just before sundown before we could turn on our lights. But during an air-raid warning, all lights had to be turned off even with the drapes closed.

That night, classes had just begun when the sirens blew, and all lights were immediately extinguished. I was only six, my older sister was thirteen, and my little sister was just two. One by one, men began to pray. I recognized each voice, and every man's prayer was rich and fervent. Then gradually, I heard a wonderful sound—the sound of one voice singing lightly and sweetly until all joined in with a swelling of love-filled rejoicing in song the likes of which I had never heard before. All of us sang filled with hope and joy in the Lord. I sang my heart out no longer afraid.

There I was sitting with my mother and father with their deep faith, my loving older sister beautiful and calm, and my baby sister asleep in total trust in Mama's arms. Mama leaned down and patted me; she told me that if anything happened to us, we were in the best place we could be, together in God's house. I was tuckered out and finally lay down with my head in Mama's lap, closed my eyes, and fell asleep to those glorious voices singing verse after verse by heart, hymn after hymn, in that close, safe dark. An indelible and actually joyous experience of my young years.

At church, week after week, I learned the dramatic, prophetic stories of the Old Testament and the soul-saving New Testament. I watched the lives of very human but very dedicated people serving the Lord year after year. Our weekly communion services were always solemn and quiet; they were one of the most important parts of our worship services. A hush fell on the audience as the communion servers in their Sunday best lined up at the communion table. We were reminded of God's Son's sacrifice as we took the bread of His body and the grape juice to commemorate the precious blood He shed for us. There we all were, totally different personalities and of varying depths of faith and backgrounds; some were calm and patient, some were feisty and loud as Peter of old had been, but then, we were united in honoring our Savior and remembering His sacrifice so we might have eternal life.

That reminds me of an experience I had in Arkansas. We were taking a long-awaited vacation there to visit relatives and revisit where Daddy had been born and raised, where Mama and Daddy had met and married, and where my older sister and I had been born. I was fifteen then, an impressionable town girl transported to a place caught in time—all dirt roads, no electricity, no gas, no running water in the house, one little general store with a single gasoline pump out front, and worst of all, no indoor bathrooms. But I saw through Daddy's eyes why he had yearned to see it again because I had never seen more beautiful, greener, and picturesque rolling hills and lush ponds.

I was privileged to spend two weeks with many relatives, but especially important was the time I spent with my father's parents, who were living in the house in which my daddy and older sister had been born.

We had a memorable experience at the tiny Noland Church of Christ where, as usual, we never missed a service. It was the little church my parents' families had attended; Mama and Daddy had attended it as well with my older sister and me for my first few months before we moved to California. It was an old building with no landscaping—just woodsy growth encroaching, bare and drafty boards on the walls, and a floor that creaked with every step. My older sister remembered Mama teaching her Sunday school lessons there. The little room held backless wooden benches that would seat at the most maybe thirty-five. The rather lackluster singing sounded thin and pitiful and was ear-assaultingly off-key.

The men who gathered to attend the communion at the Lord's Supper table were dressed in their everyday work clothes; one was in his overalls with a wide, flowered tie tucked under the collar of his blue denim work shirt. These men all looked a hundred and nine years old to me, and one of them was toothless. They all had short, high-water haircuts combed straight back wet in honor of the Lord's Day, but all looked as if they could have benefited from a hot shower, shave, and a clothes' wash and press. One had a short, straggly, greying beard with a bulge under his lip and tobacco stains from his chaw running from his lips down his jaw. Quite a contrast to Mama in her flowing summer dress and picture hat, Daddy in his sharp blue suit—all four of us in our California Sunday best accompanying our neatly attired relatives.

The crisis came when partaking of communion. It became apparent that there was only one cup used for the entire small congregation. After the blessing, I watched as each of the men pressed his lips against the cup, and when the tobacco-stained mouth slurped, I couldn't stand it any longer and squirmed in my seat. In all my fifteen years at that point, I had never thought of such a thing. I kept glancing at Mama, who sat placidly, white-gloved hands folded, her bowed head in her pretty red hat in reverent contemplation of Christ's death. In a whisper, I quietly questioned Mama about what I was seeing. She leaned toward me and whispered back consolingly, "Don't worry, honey. The Lord won't let us catch any germs while we're in His house taking the Lord's Supper."

I was not quite mollified, but I did feel marginally better when the cup passed to Mama, and she took her ever-present, lace-edged hankie and carefully wiped the entire rim of the cup before sipping, and then doing that again before handing it to me. As my daughter laughingly put it when I told her the story many years later, my mother, her Mimi, had a deep faith in the divine but a wide streak of practicality. It made me recall Mama often saying in her high, sweet voice, "The Lord helps those who help themselves."

In this, the winter of my days, I am pretty much housebound and haven't attended church services in a long time. Now on Sundays, I roll up to my kitchen table with all the big windows showcasing the big Montana panorama of God's handiwork, open my Bible, and spend a few minutes in the Word. I always reread the story of the Lord's asking us to remember Him at the Last Supper and usually always the sad telling of His Crucifixion. By myself, I pray, sometimes sing a song, and partake of a solitary communion to satisfy myself that I am obeying what He asked us to do—to remember and honor His Resurrection. I think it's important, and I feel lifted and strengthened by my short and simple act of obedience.

The worship services I hear about and watch on TV are hardly recognizable compared to the simple services I attended all my life. But I urge you that if you haven't already, find a New Testament–following, Bible-teaching home church and go! Pray for Him to direct you to the right one for you. Take your spouse or loved ones and your children, and find your niche in your own church family. The teachings and the Word of God taught week after week, year after year, will seep into your soul and benefit you and yours for all time. You will find it socially fulfilling as well, and you will have a network to fall back on when you need advice or help in times of trouble. You will work side by side with some of the funniest, hardest-working, most-dedicated people you'll ever know, and you will watch your children blossom in the Lord.

I think I've heard it all at this stage of my life—people have told me they don't attend church or quit going for many reasons, including the fact that hypocrites and all sorts of lowlifes were also members of the church. Those who believe that are right, but have they stopped buying groceries at a store because undesirables shop there? Have they stopped going to the movies because they might sit next to a lowlife? Will they refuse to go to the park or to the tennis courts or ride on the biking trails because hypocrites use them? How about Disneyland? Do you not go there because for sure there are undesirables there?

The church is not the gathering of perfected saints but a collection of those who are believers and are in all degrees of faith in their own walks. The church is full of those who seek godly lives; in their own stumbling, stop-and-start, imperfect ways, they are trying to get to heaven. I've heard the expression, "The church is a hospital for sinners." Attending worship is an act of obedience to the command of our Lord and Savior.

As you obey and attend, in your own concentration on the words of the songs sung and the prayers offered, in your absorption of the sermon's message, and in your acknowledgment of the sacred importance of communion, who knows what influence you may be having on someone who is watching you and your faithful example? He or she could be a struggling member looking to you for guidance.

So if this enriching, growing experience is not part of your life, try it. I had my ups and downs at church—at times, people disappointed me, but I also experienced tear-filled, sky-high, glorious moments there. Christ was preached and God was obeyed there, and my soul-satisfying faith was consistently strengthened throughout my life. It continues to this day to uphold me. Every worship service, every class, every fellowship, every women's event, every song practice, every home Bible class or get-together built layer upon satisfying layer of my faith, and all intertwined to make an unbreakable bond. I face eternity these days with an unshakable faith. I want that for my friends, family, and dear readers. As the old hymn says, "What a day of rejoicing that will be!" I want that for all of us.

Father, once again, in gratitude and asking forgiveness for any sin in my life either by omission or commission, please hear my prayer. If anyone reading my words is touched and nudged toward seeking You, please give Your angels charge over them to bring them to exactly where You want them to be.

Change our lives to be overwhelmingly full of You and Your will, and make Your plan clear to us. Thank You for all the faithful down through the years who taught and nurtured me. Bless all those in Your service, and make me know how to be more worthy of the name "Christian." Your will always, in His name, amen.

Heaven: What I Think It May Be Like

My Father's house has many rooms; if that were not so, would I have told you that I am going there to prepare a place for you? And if I go and prepare a place for you, I will come back and take you to be with me that you also may be where I am.

—John 14:2-3 (NIV)

I knew in an instant when the trumpet sounded its universal blast, a sound like no other, this is the day. I am on my knees, bowing with the rest of the world while unimaginable things are happening, twisting and whirling, whisking away the detritus of all I have ever known. No longer is it "The King Is Coming". Just as he promised, HE HAS COME! Filling up, welling up and spilling over all of the eastern sky, He is riding that magnificent horse. Legions of heaven's host reach more than the outer limits as far as my eye can see. There are colors unknown blasting my vision that I've never seen before, glowing over the entire sky, and undulating clouds carry singing angels, and warrior angels, and cherubs and cherubim. All of us, down below, on our knees, tremble.

The world has stopped.

All of creation is in pause.

The entire universe is in supplication, and in wonder, and in acknowledgement. Here is our King! As the prophecy of old foretold, "Every knee shall bow!"

Jesus Christ, our Lord, our Savior and our Judge.

It is that time. Will I or won't I gain the gates of heaven itself. I've confidently expected for years that I would gain eternity with Him. I've dreamed of this day, begged the Father to gather me to Himself and grant me just a little cottage in the corner of heaven. Just to be near Him, to witness the angels and to absorb every bit of ethereal goodness and beauty. To do whatever heavenly assignment is given me for all of eternity.

But, today, in my most imaginative, my wildest far-flung envisioning of life in the supernatural, I never came close to this fearful, joyous filling up and running over of my soul and spirit. Now I see what love is. Now I understand what kindness means, and know how pure in heart looks, and I am feeling so woefully lacking in what my pitiful earthly attempts at offerings were. I am so hopefully awaiting that assignment in paradise, for within me there is that empty place that only heaven can fill.

I hear an ethereal music, a chorus of harmonic voices in the exuberant singing background. I can hear the most all-encompassing, gentlest, most mesmerizing voice saying over and over again, "Welcome my good and faithful servant. Enter in and know the joys of eternal life!"

Welcome! welcome! welcome! Not once have I heard, "Attention, please, Baptists over there. Please remember, this is not your national convention." Or, "Episcopalians, pass your offering baskets a little more to the left please." Or, "Methodists, please be seated for a special guest and his musical offering." Or, "Church of Christers, please take your casseroles to the far gate." Actually, all I hear is welcome, welcome servants!

Now, in deep, clear and vibrant tones that momentarily rivet me to my spot, a voice that sends chills from the top of my head to the tip of my toes, I hear that gentle beckoning, "Jolita, welcome home, my good and faithful servant. Enter into all that heaven holds."

Somehow, I thought there would be a loud party-like atmosphere, happy hollers of discovery, and running and throwing arms around one another, and talking all at once. For me, it is just all of a sudden being there, in the midst of the most normal, quiet, relaxed familiarity. There is the peace of hundreds of children laughing and giggling, and I look up to see them skipping and running and turning cartwheels on indescribably green rolling hills.

I feel a strong arm slide around my waist and look up into Bill's smiling brown eyes, and I melted into him as if we had never been apart. Mama and Daddy are right there, holding hands, each reaching out with their free arms beckoning me to them. Our Shelley Ann stands separate, laughing and laughing at me, one arm sweeping her blowing blonde hair off her face. Tiffany walks up, her gorgeous smile shining, ducking her head in her old familiar gesture, and reaches out to take Shelley's hand. My Gramma and Grampa Sullivan look youthful and vigorous, and just wait quietly, shyly smiling and expectant. There's my Papa and Mama Penn, tiny people as always, vital and happy. I see a whole cluster of Sullivans, my aunts and uncles calmly waiting. Right beside them, the Penn Family chattering and smiling, that Penn energy just oozing into the atmosphere, and my Aunt Addie throws back her head in her "tickled-to-pieces" familiar laughter. I'm thrilled to see Mary Jean, my childhood best friend, slim and girlish, dark hair curling about her beloved face, quietly standing with her mother and father and a host of the Ellis family, all sending their welcome smiles directly my way. Arvella and her precious mother are watching me, and I gasp in delight and wonder at the sight of my precious old friend. I am aware of so many more loved ones stretching far into the distance, a quietly laughing crowd, and I know I'll get to visit with every single beloved in this home of infinity.

Suddenly I am aware of my Bill standing quietly by me, looking maybe thirty years old, and in his arms, two darling babies seriously contemplating me. I am struck silent. Instantly I know these two little ones who were never born, yet still part of us, a huge part of me, and I rejoice and stroke their silky cheeks, realizing they were never lost, just waiting for this reunion.

There are Bill's family, so many McDaniels that I never met on earth, and our beloved church family. J.B. peeks at me from between the milling crowd and points straight at me, huge smile from ear to ear and says, "Hi Joey! We made it, honey!" More beloved faces smile and wave at me. I hear an old familiar squeak right in my ear, and, for once I don't jump, startled. I turn to look up into the bluest of ice blue eyes crinkling at me, and it's my beloved Hale, dark curly hair falling over his face like JoAn always loved. He leans over and presses his forehead up against mine. That's all, just a quiet affirmation of his love for me. There are rows upon rows of neighbors, loving friends, more loved ones than I can imagine, and here we are, all of us together, waiting our call to our spot in eternity.

I began to have a glimmer of understanding that no matter how long our journey was on earth, it was never long enough to be truly together. We always had a schedule. I'm thinking that this wonderful serene welcome I'm experiencing is part of our reward, no nerve-jangling rushing or yelling or frantic grabbing for those precious fleeting moments we could never retrieve in our world. Now we have forever to be together, to participate in our part of praising our Father, getting to know angels who protected us and our families, and finding out what our jobs will be while in these lofty, unearthly spheres - seeking out those ancient forefathers of ours for unhurried visits, and telling impetuous Peter how we understand.

And finally, the long-awaited ultimate reward of face-to-face with Jesus himself. Will He let me hug Him? Will He hold my hand looking lovingly into my eyes giving me my own special moment? Will He present the Holy Spirit in recognizable form so we can thank Him for a thousand comforts and guidances?

And so, loving the reunion, and as we wait to get our assignments, I look around the entrance to my long-awaited, long-hoped for heavenly home. I began to finally actually see the magnificence of much more than the precious pearls and jewels and gold lining the streets and in the distance the far-off shining city. I see the iridescence of the promised crystal river flowing freely and notice a stunningly lovely tree spreading out its lush canopy over the banks. There, to my thrilled surprise, leisurely stretched out on the grass lay Pooky, Freckles and her puppies, Janjolou, Tom, Cleo and Pansy and all their kittens, the elegant Sing Su, and finally little Tinkerbelle who sits looking straight at me, straining towards me for all she is worth. But Scarlett, little Lady Scarlett isn't as disciplined. She can't stand it one more minute. She bounces her tiny body across the most unbelievably soft green grass right to my ankles rubbing her little three-and-a-half pound self, back and forth, back and forth, until I pick her up and bury my face in her soft, sweet-smelling fur. It is just, well, the only word is heavenly.

So, yes, you know and I know this probably isn't the way heaven will be at all. It's probably just my vision because of my beliefs and my somewhat limited studies, and probably a lot of hoping and longing.

But, at my stage of life, heaven occupies a lot of my thinking, mostly because so very many of my loved ones are there already, and then, the most obvious, I am sooner there than not.

But if this little imaginary trip causes even one of my readers to think about where he or she will spend eternity, and change the direction their life might be taking, it was well worth the time it took to read this flight of fancy! God bless us all, and yes, may we all meet in heaven, the angels around us.

As always, Father God, in Your great mercy and love, thank You for the hope of heaven, and that we can trust Your Son's judgment about our lives. Please forgive us of any and all that would keep us from heaven, and bring us home to You for an eternity of praising and serving You and being with our loved ones. Your will be done always, in Jesus' name, amen.

Quiet Nights

But at the beginning of creation God "made them male and female." For this reason a man will leave his father and mother and be united to his wife, and the two will become one flesh. So they are no longer two, but one flesh. Therefore what God has joined together, let no one separate.

—Mark 10:6–9 (NIV)

On May 7, 1955, my prince and I stood in the little wedding chapel, Capilla de San Antonio in Anaheim, California, and were united in marriage witnessed by about fifty of our loving friends and family. We were married fifty-four years before he left for his forever home. I wrote this not long after. I miss him today as sharply as the night I wrote this, though I am ever so grateful he is at peace and whole and happy. Some of you will relate.

When nights are long
And sleep is short,
I long for you
To come to me.

I listen to the quiet.
Not one night bird warbles.
Every leaf on every oak
Holds its breath.

An acorn drops,
The sound so soft

A sleeping squirrel doesn't
Lift its head.

Through our years,
Quiet nights were friendly,
Knowing soon I'd hear
Your footfall down the hall.

Your soft, tired words soothed me.
Our "good nights, sleep tights,"
Your deep throaty chuckles,
All muttled by our thick, warm comforter.

Now, I only hear my heartbeat
Thumping in my ears.
Now, a tiny creak,
My home's old age protesting.

Your comfy chair's no longer there,
For in the cool of night
The leather sighed and whispered,
A sad reminder you left me.

Perhaps I should have kept it,
Letting your cushions surround me
Absorbing any lingering essence of you,
Sinking into the comfort of pretense.

But the vision of it waiting,
Newspapers stacked beside,
Your table ready with your cup,
No, I could not abide your empty chair.

This long night, this quiet night,
I know the hour the fog steals in
By the creeping chill settling so silently
On my back and around my ankles.

Outside, the dark hides grey shrouds of mist
Hanging like Spanish moss among the branches,
And little birds and furry critters hunker down

Thankful daylight is still far beyond our back hill.

My bed is waiting, but you are not.
Nights are longer, sleep is shorter.
I long for you, my darling,
To come to me, and you do not.

I close my eyes, pull up the comforter,
When just an echo, a past remembrance really,
Of your warm, sweet breath softly sighs,
"Good night, sweetie," and I sleep.

My prince was very encouraging about my painting and writing; he teasingly called me "Mrs. Rembrandt." He was my biggest cheerleader. When I had a stroke several years ago, he was Johnny-on-the-spot. I think he did most of the dishes and cooking for about a year. We were all naturally frightened, but he especially took it very hard. One afternoon, he came to my hospital bedside, sat beside me, and put his head down on the bed. Taking my hand, he wept and said, "Oh, Jo, your beautiful mind. Please God, bring back her beautiful mind. Please God."

Thank You, my Lord God, for answering my husband's prayer, for giving us fifty-four wonderful years, and for granting me an even longer and richer life.

My prince was in the space industry, and nothing would have completed his life more than a ride on one of the rockets he so many times helped fling into the heavens. His was a dangerous job, and he himself had enough miraculous escapes, which just solidified his belief in God and in angels forever.

We both loved the night sky, and we spent many a rewarding hour watching the movement of the stars, the moon in all its enchanting stages, and the passing twinkling satellites he had been a part of. He was a man's man, one of energy and passion, always looking to the future but gentle enough to soothe a baby. He was overflowing with love enough to seal my heart with his for a lifetime. He was my own living, breathing angel.

I am praying for my readers who want to be blessed with someone at least as fulfilling for their lives—their own angels. The light of his life was the incandescence of my existence. That brilliance was taken away, and there remains a pall over my life that doesn't lift. God has given me much, and I am grateful for the joy and the unexpected pleasure of the work He planned for me, but I don't expect that special light my prince cast to be reignited until we meet again. I do hold dear to my heart that beautiful hope and expectation!

He was not a Shakespeare kind of guy, but he indulged me. At his memorial, I thought it fitting to have Shakespeare's immortal words read, words that always make me melt, and I'm including them here.

> *When he shall die, take him and cut him out into little stars and he shall make the face of heaven so fine that all the world will be in love with night and pay no worship to the garish sun.*

On Being Me

I wrote a synopsis about my life a couple of years ago that I want you to remember me by.

> *There is a time for everything,*
> *and a season for every activity under the heavens:*
> *a time to be born and a time to die,*
> *a time to plant and a time to uproot,*
> *a time to kill and a time to heal,*
> *a time to tear down and a time to build,*
> *a time to weep and a time to laugh,*
> *a time to mourn and a time to dance,*
> *a time to scatter stones and a time to gather them,*
> *a time to embrace and a time to refrain from embracing,*
> *a time to search and a time to give up,*
> *a time to keep and a time to throw away,*
> *a time to tear and a time to mend,*
> *a time to be silent and a time to speak,*
> *a time to love and a time to hate,*
> *a time for war and a time for peace.*
>
> *—Ecclesiastes 3:1–8 (NIV)*

When you think of me, if you think of me at all,
Think of me laughing, please, and my giggle.
Think of my quick smile, and my sometimes hiding it
Because my sense of humor is tickled at what perhaps

Would not amuse anyone else at all.
At my laughing at my own foibles,
And at the posturing of human beings
Acting out our foolishments before our Creator.
Think of me at nine years old,
Barefoot, skinny, tomboy,
Dirty shorts and scabbed knees,
Pedaling hard on my old, junkyard bike
Not even out of breath
Nimbly running up the old leaning tree,
Clambering out on its rough, forked branches,
So grandly surveying my small neighborhood
     from such a lofty view.

Picture blond, straight, short hair cut in a Dutch-boy bob
On a little tomboy with skinned elbows,
     dirty feet, and bitten nails.
That was me hunkered over a game of marbles,
Playing with a bunch of little boys squatting in the dirt.
My little sister, sun-browned, serene, long, dark
     curls damply curling on her neck,
Watching and admiring, waiting patiently for me to finish.
See me digging in a pocket, hoping to find
     a nickel or shaking her piggy bank
So we could buy a Popsicle to share in the
     shade if the ice cream truck came by.

Out of we three girls, I was the one in the family then
Whoever broke a bone, or had to have stitches.
Wasn't I proud to be the one to whom
     Daddy pitched his old baseball?
Didn't I puff up my chest hearing him brag to Mama
How he "burned" in the ball, and I didn't flinch,
     never letting on how bad it hurt?
For I was Daddy's "boy" at the time, who
     listened to the ballgame with him,
Who watched him change the oil in
     the car and patch tires,
Who followed him around as he mowed the
     lawn and "helped" him by raking leaves.

Watch a little girl walk forward, knees shaking,
To tentatively but courageously commit and
      be baptized at nine years old.
See her young and vulnerable heart,
And know that I was that little girl,
      repentant and awestruck,
Frightened and determined.
Remember this of me: my early
      commitment never wavered,
And through my weakness, through my human curiosity,
In spite of my many wayward thoughts and
      some occasional unwise choices,
My cornerstone, my rock never failed—
He was and is my God.

Remember that my tender heart, all
      those years ago, loved,
And oh, how I still love,
The shine of dew on dandelions sparkling in the sun,
Back then, one arm thrown around my little sissie,
The two of us searching the lawn, picking
      a yellow bouquet for Mama.
Years later, cloud-watching with my
      own little ones around me,
Flat on our backs,
Blades of grass tickling our legs and
      scratching our sunburns.
So much fun watching shapes in the sky
      forming funny little sheep, kitty cats,
Old, bent men with wispy beards, and
      a towering castle in the sky.

Remember me as a fifteen-year-old
      wildly in love with the piano,
Practicing as much as three-hour stretches,
Especially in the night after listening to
      a soaring classical concert,
Tenderly offering up Claire de Lune, and
      somberly rendering Moonlight Sonata.
Today, as clear as if it were yesterday,
I hear the sound of Mama's silver scissors

Snipping and cutting out lovely fabric for our dresses.
The ones we dared not touch to cut anything,
And I have them today in my sewing basket.
Picture me in pin curls, forcing my short,
    straight hair into soft waves,
And my older sister patiently painting my still bitten nails,
Shepherding me toward oncoming womanhood.

When you see blue, pale, deep or medium,
    aqua blue, ocean blue,
The forever blue of the sky,
Remember that it is and always has
    been my favorite color.
Calming, peaceful, deep-blue velvet of night,
Diamonds sparkling against the deep dark.
Remember (or imagine) me in my size-eight,
    royal-blue, velvet sheath dress!
With shiny little satin bows on the sleeves
    and over the slits in the skirt,
And a matching velvet-and-satin stole I made myself.
Imagine my heart melting
When my prince rolled his warm brown
    eyes and said, "Wow!"

So, through my favorites, like down on
    my knees playing jacks;
Reading *Black Beauty* and *Little Women*,
    Charlotte Brontë and Jane Austen;
Through bowling and tennis, skating and
    cycling, embroidery and knitting;
Through our love story, through rocking babies,
    baking cakes and roasting turkeys;
Through packing lunches and homework, fevers
    and surgeries, ballet and baseball;
Through emergencies and weddings, and
    grandbabies and great-grandbabies;
And retirement and painting, illness and
    injury, death and dying;
Remember me, please, as more than the
    wobbly old woman in her chair.

For long ago, my hair was gold and shiny in the sun,
And once, my legs ran the mile to school, and I didn't tire.
And my Prince Charming came and
    stayed and fulfilled our forever,
And I woke at dawn listening, relishing sounds
    of babies cooing in their cribs.
Friends, family, and worship,
The lilting Chopin and commanding Beethoven of my life.

So when you think of me, if you do,
Though my hair is more silver now than gold,
Please remember me laughing,
Still as much the tomboy with scabby
    knees who climbed the tree,
As I am the shaky grammy who sits
    and knits and praises God,
For He is still my God,
Forever my Great I AM.

Poem—"God the Artist," by Angela Morgan

Here is one of my favorite poems by Angela Morgan to leave you with.

"God the Artist"

God, when you thought of a pine tree,
How did you think of a star?
How did you dream of the Milky Way
To guide us from afar.
How did you think of a clean brown pool
Where flecks of shadows are?
God, when you thought of a cobweb,
How did you think of dew?
How did you know a spider's house
Had shingles bright and new?
How did you know the human folk
Would love them like they do?

God, when you patterned a bird song,
Flung on a silver string,
How did you know the ecstasy
That crystal call would bring?
How did you think of a bubbling throat
And a darling speckled wing?

God, when you chiseled a raindrop,
How did you think of a stem,
Bearing a lovely satin leaf
To hold the tiny gem?
How did you know a million drops
Would deck the morning's hem?

Why did you mate the moonlit night
With the honeysuckle vines?
How did you know Madeira bloom
Distilled ecstatic wines?
How did you weave the velvet disk
Where tangled perfumes are?
God, when you thought of a pine tree,
How did you think of a star?

finale

It is with a sigh of satisfaction and a little tug of regret that I find this book is finished. I'm going to miss the nudges in my mind that made me run to my computer to—*Quick!*—get my insistent thoughts down on paper, many of which were surprises even to me. I thank the Holy Spirit, who prompted me, and I thank You, dear Father, for allowing this to come to fruition.

After my move to Montana in my old age, I wondered what He had planned for me. I prayed He would send me a mission, one I would recognize and could actually accomplish. On Easter Sunday, 2017, *bang!*—the idea for this book presented itself to me and insisted it be written.

My goal was to lovingly offer these essays—the long and short and in-between ones—to uplift and encourage my readers and help them discover joy and laughter in daily living. I hoped to maybe spark a remembrance in my readers' lives that might bring them warmth and love and the desire to keep on keeping on.

Also, I want my children, my grandchildren, and eventually my great-grandchildren to know who their mom, their grammy, or their Gigi Jo truly was and is and add my background history that perhaps they did not know.

When they read this, if they didn't already, they will know the way to eternal salvation. I pray my words will help them and all my readers to be inspired and to seek out for themselves who God is and His way. I want them to remember that I was so blessed with a happy life, yes, sometimes with ups and down, but one full and rewarding. Through the bumpy parts, with God's help all along the way, I recovered from some of life's scariest, most devastating crashes, even from losing their Daddy-o, their Uncle Bill, their grumpaw.

I also want them and my readers to know that they too have what it takes and can do it too. I am ready for God to take me home any time He wants, but if He has something else for me to do, I'm up for that also!

I pray that God will send you an angel, one who will change your life with His blessed message of good news, and you will be forever different and forever joyous.

This is the end of now but the beginning of forever. Once more, in love and in all sincerity, God bless you, dear readers, and angels around every one of you!

Father God, thank You for this opportunity, and in Your holy wisdom, please place this book in hands that need whatever good they may glean from it. Always, all to Your glory, in Jesus's name, amen.

Made in the USA
San Bernardino, CA
02 April 2018